PENGUIN BOOKS

LAUGH, I THOUGHT I'D DIE

A former logger from British Columbia, Dennis Kaye came to national attention as The Incredible Shrinking Man when his letters to Peter Gzowski were read aloud on CBC Radio's "Morningside." Gzowski convinced Kaye to keep writing, and for two years he typed laboriously, one key at a time, with a wand attached to his head. He and his wife, Ruth, live on Quadra Island with their two daughters, Rebecca and Michalla.

AF271347

Laugh, I Thought I'd Die

My Life with ALS

DENNIS KAYE

Penguin Books

PENGUIN BOOKS
Published by the Penguin Group
Penguin Books Canada Ltd, 10 Alcorn Avenue, Toronto, Ontario,
Canada M4V 3B2
Penguin Books Ltd, 27 Wrights Lane, London W8 5TZ, England
Penguin Books USA Inc., 375 Hudson Street, New York, New York
10014, U.S.A.
Penguin Books Australia Ltd, Ringwood, Victoria, Australia
Penguin Books (NZ) Ltd, 182-190 Wairau Road, Auckland 10,
New Zealand

Penguin Books Regsitered Offices: Harmondsworth, Middlesex, England

First published in Viking by Penguin Books Canada Limited, 1993

Published in Penguin Books, 1994

10 9 8 7 6 5 4 3 2 1

Some of the information found in Part Two is taken from brochures published by the Amyotrophic Lateral Sclerosis Society of Canada and the
Amyotrophic Lateral Sclerosis Society of Ontario. This information is used
by permission.

Manufactured in Canada

Canadian Catloguing in Publication Data
Kaye, Dennis, 1955-
   Laugh, I thought I'd die

ISBN 0-14-023570-1

1. Kaye, Dennis, 1955-   -Health 2. Amyotrophic lateral sclerosis - Patients
- Canada - Biography. I. Title

RC405.A24K38 1993   362.1'9683   C93-094950-1

This book is dedicated

to my wife, Ruth,

for her quiet strength,

unfailing devotion,

and for the best rhubarb mousse

west of Heart's Content.

Preface

A couple of summers ago, as I'm sure he'll tell you, Dennis Kaye and what he calls his "small but unstoppable circle of friends" decided to hold an art auction to raise some money to fight ALS, the disease that, if it has its way, will one day kill him.

No one thought they could bring it off.

I had my own doubts, I'll confess now, even though I thought I knew Dennis pretty well by then, and even though he had somehow managed to con me into putting a welcome to the prospective buyers onto an audio tape, which they played when the curtain rose. They did better than, I think, even they had dared to hope, raising $20,000, and, I'm sure, their spirits and their confidence. Dennis wrote to me:

"It would be juvenile of me to gloat, so, instead, to all the naysayers, I offer these timeless words of profundity and wisdom—Na na, na na na."

I feel a bit the same about this book.

I met Dennis, if that is the word (we've still never been in the same room), in the winter of 1988-89. He faxed me at

"Morningside," the CBC radio program where I work. "My name is Dennis Kaye," his letter began. "I'm just over five foot ten with brown hair and blue eyes. I like to think of myself as an okay guy, but unfortunately, at thirty-four years old, I'm dying…"

I'm not sure what triggered that first communication. "Morningside" is a daily three-hour mixture of everything from interviews to recipes, and people write to it for all kinds of reasons. Sometimes they're responding to something (or someone) they've heard on the air. But just as often, as with Dennis, they simply want to get something off their chests.

Dennis went on:

"The vast majority of people with my condition last three years or less, so you could say that, in my fourth year, I'm on the home stretch…"

I looked ahead at the typed closing. "The Incredible Shrinking Man," it said. The signature was a scrawl, all but illegible. Even then, it turned out, he was laboriously working at a keyboard with a wand attached to his forehead. Handwriting was beyond him, but the writing was as clear as a brook.

"Does the name Muscular Dystrophy ring a bell?" the fax went on. "How about Multiple Sclerosis? Of course they do. These names and others…"

By now, I was caught up. The strength and clarity of the style, the force and the feeling of the arguments, and, most of all, the wry humour that shines through even his most bitter paragraphs—"the fact is, a terminal diagnosis can ruin your whole day"—carried me on. Though I didn't know it at the time, a relationship—a friendship, I dared to call it in a column I once wrote—had begun.

Since then I've tried to keep up with him. He's written when he's felt like it, or, from time to time, when "Morningside" has asked him to comment on some public issue. I've treasured all his letters, and I've come to treasure him, too; he is a special and inspiring man.

When he told me, a year or so ago, that he was going to continue to write in the way he had written to me, and even to incorporate some of his letters into the book that would come out of it all, I no longer had any doubt. He *would* finish, I knew, and send his book across the country like an angry—and funny—flare of courage.

And here it is. Dennis's work. Na na, na na na.

We're all dying, you know, and have been since the day we burst the womb.

Dennis is just doing it more meaningfully than the rest of us.

Peter Gzowski
September 1993

Introduction

W e walked side by side until the trail became too narrow. After passing close behind a lighthouse, the pathway widened and we rejoined hands. Taking four steps to my one, but keeping pace, was my youngest daughter, Michalla. I didn't feel much like talking, which suited her just fine. The ability to carry both sides of a conversation seems to be a common trait for three-year-olds, and likewise, for Michalla, silence was a sworn enemy.

Her hand felt small and warm. Mine was cold, and her holding it stopped it from flopping about like so much processed meat. Since my diagnosis two years before, my right arm and hand had become all but useless, and to those who didn't know me, this paralysis was all that betrayed my condition. Balanced on my left shoulder was a camera tripod. I'd started out carrying it in my left hand, but as usual, my grip had quickly weakened. Like the right arm, my left was growing weaker by the day, and denial of the disease's progress was becoming increasingly futile. It was 1987 and the odds were, in a year, it would all be over.

A quarter mile or so further brought us out to a wind-swept cape, bordered by an exposed stretch of tidal boulders. Cape Mudge, the southernmost tip of Quadra Island, juts its rocky chin into the northernmost reaches of Georgia Strait, offering an unobstructed and unbeatable view down the open Gulf. Just out from shore, dozens of anglers flitted about on high-speed sanpans, while far off in the distance, Denman and Hornby Islands clung precariously to the edge of the earth.

I'd only agreed to bring my daughter after repeated bleatings of "Pleeease daddy," and even then, her coming along required the solemn promise that, no matter what, she was to be a "big girl." So, as Michalla frightened nearby seagulls with her desperate and high-pitched need to return home, I did my best to block out everything but the sun, the scenery and that summery smell of ocean. As hands of wind combed the tall grass around us, I remember envying her for releasing so easily that which I found so difficult. Once her wailing had subsided to a low continuous moan, she gazed up through tear-filled eyes and gradually wore me down. We went home early.

If someone had told me then that four years later I would start writing a book on the high-points and pitfalls that await the terminally ill, I'd have laughed in their face. There's no shortage of books telling us how we should live, but nowhere could I find a comprehensive manual on how to die. Even though a few hundred million people do it every year, there is no guide...no accurate map or list of instructions. Researching the subject was by no means easy. Sure, there's been a lot of discussion lately on euthanasia and "dying with dignity," but strangely enough, the field's real experts aren't available for comment. And even if they were, I lack the lofty morals to preach or pass judgment on issues so personal. I have no degrees in psychology or theology, but several years on diagnostic death row have convinced me that some people could really use a practical, non-sectarian overview of what to expect.

My future may still be doubtful, but in the here and now, this book is intended to accomplish three things. Hopefully, it will help smooth the emotional road for people who, like myself, face the daily uncertainty of a terminal condition. More importantly, I like to think that it might serve to inspire others who, for whatever reason, deem their situations less than perfect. Finally, I hope that sorting through what's been happening to me will better prepare me for what eventually will. The way I see it right now, my life is a lot like that afternoon out on the Cape. I'm really just going home early.

Contents

Part
One

The Preliminary Stuff

In my dreams I climb the mountains high,

In my dreams I face the samurai.

In my dreams I stroke my lover's hair,

In my dreams I travel everywhere.

In my dreams I kiss and never tell,

In my dreams I'm not a languid shell.

In my dreams I never convalesce,

In my dreams I don't have ALS.

I didn't always have ALS.
In fact for a while I led a life
that some would envy.

1

Unfettered Times

They called it "the Sched" short for Scheduled Flight, and you could hear it coming a mile away. On British Columbia's wilderness coast in the seventies, it was an ancient, single-prop de Havilland Otter that coughed and sputtered its way from Phillips Arm to Rivers Inlet on a sort of camp-by-camp milk-run. Each day, but never on the same route twice, the Sched would fly out of Campbell River, picking up and dropping off loggers, road-builders, survey-ors, bush-bound Natives and anyone else who lived or worked beyond the end of the road. More times than I can remember, I watched the Sched taxi in, unload people or freight, taxi out and take off, but one particular delivery I'll never forget.

It was the spring of 1978 and I was one of only two contractors who made up the entire workforce of a small gyppo camp at the head of a beautiful mainland inlet called Port Neville. "Gyppo," for those who don't know, is the name given to a dying group of small, independent, often haywire logging operations that at one time dotted the B.C. coast. I was leasing a rubber-tired skidder, an all-terrain machine used for dragging logs out of the woods, and on this particular day I'd come off the hill early to meet the afternoon Sched. A newly hired employee was supposed to be on board, so after the Otter took off, if all went well, my payroll would rise by one. Not counting me, this would swell the ranks of my fledgling forestry empire to a crew of two.

Up until that fateful day, a single employee and I had been living the bachelor life. I'll be the first to admit that falling trees all day can leave one with an appetite for eating food…but not for preparing it. Although my faller, a French Canadian named Pierre, knew his way around the kitchen, he was getting really tired of doubling as cook. And likewise, I was getting pretty sick of ending my dawn-to-dusk days doubling as the camp's dishwashing housekeeper. Since the last cook quit, we had endured this thankless drudgery for six agonizing days, and enough was enough.

I considered myself a fair-minded employer, so a few nights earlier, over a quart of tequila, I'd called our first grievance meeting to order. The only item on the agenda was tabled, and minutes later the deciding ballot was cast. I abstained, being management and all, and so, as you might have guessed, the decision was unanimous: hire a cook. With our most urgent problem so easily solved, we finished off both the evening and the tequila to one of Pierre's fist-pounding renditions of "Sholitaridy Frrrever."

I reached camp just as the familiar floatplane was touching down and I walked out the stiff-leg to greet our new cook.

For the benefit of the uninitiated, a stiff-leg is a makeshift sidewalk, two or three logs wide, that boats and planes tie to. You might think of it as a kind of floating hitching rail. Ours was slippery in spots, but for the most part was roughened by years of chalked boot traffic.

The plane's weather-worn propeller ticked to a stop and a plain-clothed pilot dropped onto the pontoon. We exchanged pleasantries while the plane quietly drifted the last few feet toward me. When I reached up to grab the passing wing strut, I caught sight of a young woman staring out one of the small, round windows. As she surveyed the derelict old barges that I affectionately called home, her unguarded expression betrayed exactly what she was thinking: "What in hell have I gotten myself into?"

After handing me a bulging packsack, the pilot helped his passenger to dockside, then gave his plane a calculated push and climbed back into the cockpit. Before we'd even had a chance to exchange names, our voices were cut short by the reluctant whine of the aircraft coming back to life. It taxied to the end of the stiff-leg, turned hard to windward and accelerated.

Then the strangest thing happened. A couple days earlier, I'd spotted a stray log drifting by. It was just a low-floating little hemlock but worth a few bucks, so I'd thrown a line on it. It was only tied up at one end, and the incoming tide had just started to slowly swing it away from the stiff-leg.

To this day, I have no idea what possessed her to do it, but without so much as a wink or a nod, my new cook stepped onto the loose log and started walking. The little low-floater floated a little lower. Yelling at the top of my lungs, I tried to point out her mistake, but the stubborn old de Havilland, still reaching for air, drowned out every living thing in Port Neville. Maybe she was just frazzled from her first ride in a floatplane (sometimes they can be pretty hairy). Maybe she hoped to somehow catch the plane before it lifted off. I don't know for sure, but about twenty feet out she suddenly saw the error of her ways and froze. A few seconds later the plane broke free, banked left and disappeared behind a tree-lined point. Finally, with the Sched gone, gently lapping waves were all that broke the silence.

If you've ever been on a free-floating log, you know that walking isn't really that hard. The tricky part for most folks is getting turned around without falling in, and my new cook showed no sign of attempting the latter without help. I reassured her as best I could and gingerly stepped out onto the log. The little low-floater floated a little lower. Her long, straight, dark-brown hair hung almost to her waist, and as I worked my way toward her, I remember thinking how close it was to getting a salt-water rinse. I took her hand, and as she cautiously turned to face me, I couldn't help but notice the unsettled look on her pretty, freckled face. Without making any sudden moves, Ruth and I introduced ourselves.

Right about here, you're most likely expecting us to go ass over tea-kettle, but we didn't. Short careful step by short careful step, we made our way back to the relative safety of the stiff-leg and paused a second for Ruth to collect herself. In small talk, she told me that, despite the inlet's deceiving calm, her flight had been rough, which probably accounted for her feelings of disorientation. At any rate, in no time she regained her composure and was ready to head for shore. I shouldered her packsack, and moments later my new cook was standing safely on dry land.

Now you're probably wondering why, if we never fell in, I would consider this an unforgettable experience. Well, I had no way of knowing it then, but taking Ruth's hand that day turned out to be a sign of things to come. In time, I would hold her hand in romance, marriage, and more than once in childbirth (not necessarily in that order). I also had no way of knowing that, all too soon, Ruth would be coaxing me along, short, careful step by short, careful step. For the time being, though, on two strong legs, I walked Ruth around her new surroundings.

Hearing myself, in my thirties, saying that those days of gyppo logging were "the good old days" seems a bit strange, but for me, they truly were. Through the seventies, I worked in several logging camps, but the one that really seemed to mass-produce memories was a tiny transient camp owned by my father. Tiny, because it seldom employed more than six or eight people at any one time. And transient, because it never stayed in one place for more than a year or so. Whenever we finished a claim, we'd gingerly refloat that decrepit pair of wooden scows, tow them to yet another remote cove or inlet and beach them once again. When I look back now, it seems miraculous that barges so old could survive any move, let alone repeated ones. No one knew their exact age, but they were rumoured to have been built by an elderly shipwright just before a great flood. Come to think of it, there were two holes in the shop roof. Maybe that's where the giraffes stood.

If variety is the spice of life, then life on those rickety old relics was a bucket full of Tabasco-soaked chili peppers. Unlike the mind-numbing monotony I found at big union camps, every day could be counted on for at least one surprise. Admittedly, the pay was no hell, and conditions were questionable—no, tolerable—no, actually, Dad's camp barely met political prisoner guidelines set out by the Geneva Convention! But whatever it lacked in amenities, it made up for in spice. You just never got bored.

Dad never spent much time in camp, and as a rule, most of the crew were contractors, so up until I started contracting myself, I was often the only real "company" employee. This meant being continuously called on to fill whichever role was most needed at the time. Sometimes I'd stick to one job for a month or more. Other times, I could start a day bucking logs on the landing and end it on a boomboat, or cooking, or loading logs, or falling trees, or driving skidder, or swinging wrenches, or building road, or, or, or... Regardless of the job, each one came with its own gyppo-centric set of idiosyncrasies—even jobs as seemingly predictable as driving a truck.

A truck is a truck is a truck, unless of course it's a Honey Pie. Our beloved Honey Pie was to logging trucks what the abacus is to the pocket calculator. The sculptured steel nameplate welded into her grille-guard said "Sterling," but a more up-to-date brand name would have been "Sterling-Spicer-Cummins-Mack-Kenworth." Since rolling off the assembly line in 1947, virtually every piece of that grease-splattered, battle-scarred bucket-a-bolts had either been repaired, removed or replaced. Long before my time, she'd been stripped of her antiquated drive chain (that's right—a drive chain), and thanks to a wondrous new invention known in mechanical circles as a drive shaft, all her eighteen mismatched wheels turned in relative unison. As for her humungous off-highway frame, it had been altered, patched and spot-welded so often that some of us thought of her jokingly as industrial art.

My affair with Honey Pie lasted almost long enough to be considered a steady job. Each day I would climb up to the cab, grab a can of starting fluid, walk out on the fender and, with the methodic skill of a seasoned junkie, administer her morning fix. Ironically, the one thing that could wake old Honey Pie up was a liberal snort of ether (an aerosol fluid used to start stubborn diesel engines). The ritual was always the same; shoot a healthy blast up Honey's breather, jump in the cab, yank the compression release, hit the start switch, floor the throttle and commence platitudes. *Nice* truck, *good* truck, *please* truck. At first, she would only cough out thin wisps of exhaust, but gradually, as her flywheel gained momentum, wisps would turn into rhythmic puffs. *Nice* truck, *good* truck, *please* truck. Puff by puff, an ominous black cloud would build and grow until finally, Honey Pie would spring to life like some long-dormant volcano. And heralding her resurrection came an unmuffled, ear-piercing roar that would scatter seabirds and pucker pine-cones for miles around. Then, rising like a phoenix from the smoke and ash, we'd turn from the beach and begin our assault on "the hill."

About four miles out, "the hill" rose almost straight up from the valley floor. Getting to the top rarely posed a problem, but coming back down with a full load of logs was an entirely different story. As hills go, it wasn't really that long (maybe a quarter mile), but Honey Pie lacked one essential feature—brakes. Gradual slopes were safe enough, but bringing Honey Pie up to snuff for the hill would have meant the time and expense of resurfacing every last one of her worn-out brake drums. When it came to hauling logs, my Dad had an interesting philosophy. He maintained that brakes were only necessary if you planned on stopping, so until modern mechanics came up with a way of rebuilding brakes while wheels were still turning, I was to keep on truckin'.

Anyway, I can't remember who came up with the idea, but it was a real doozy. From the turn of the century, Port Neville had been home to several species of *lumberjackus erectus*. From the days of ox teams and corduroy roads, through the steam era, and right up to the introduction of high-speed grapple yarders, loggers had come and loggers had gone. Remnants of their passing were scattered around the valley like the spoils of some long-forgotten war, and as luck would have it, the solution to Honey Pie's brake problems came in the form of one of these remnants. Meandering in and out of the underbrush along the main road, it lay in wait like a great steel snake, five thousand feet of discarded skyline (a heavy cable used in days gone by to move logs aerially over long distances) left over from the days of whistle punks and steel wheels.

The plan was simple. Drag one end of the mile-long cable to the top of the hill and splice an eye. Go to the bottom of the hill, cut the cable off and splice another eye. Then flop the end of the cable over a big stump at the top of the hill, and strong-arm the eye into a shackle on the end of Honey Pie's trailer.

Are you starting to get the picture? In theory, the sheer weight of the cable, along with the brute friction of it passing around the stump, would slow me down. As I came down the hill, the opposite end would pass me on its way up, and when I reached the bottom I'd just unhook the cable and head for the beach. Next trip, the other eye would be waiting for me at the top of the hill.

To begin with, everything worked like a charm. The problem was, it would eventually work too well. I suppose I should have seen it coming, but like most loggers, it took a couple good raps on the hard-hat just to get my attention. The real tip-off should have come when it took a front-end loader, a D7 Cat and the threat of high explosives just to get the cable out of the ditch. When the West Coast rainforest wraps its tentacles around something, it rarely lets go without a fight, but with a little perseverance and a lot of ripe language, we successfully wrestled the cable into submission. Once we had its two-inch diameter carcass laid out on the hard-packed road surface like a big-game trophy, the D7 got it moving and kept it moving (barely). The great steel snake hissed in protest all the way to the top of the hill.

Once we cut the cable to length and spliced the eyes, all that remained was the procurement of a suitably skookum stump. Standing like a gift at the crest of the hill was a towering old-growth fir, and after a few minutes with a power-saw we were ready to roll.

I built a light load for the first trip down and hardly even had to tickle the brakes. In fact, I didn't need the tractor brakes at all. However, after a couple weeks of running first one way and then the other, the cable's sawing motion began to bury it further and further into the stump. With the claim almost finished, and the stump at least five feet across, I wasn't worried about the gash going right through, but the deeper the cable got, the harder it got to pull. Thinking back now, it all seems too ridiculous. With two transmissions and twenty gears to choose from, there I was, facing straight down with my boots in the basement, pulling like there was no tomorrow.

I should mention that when I was in my twenties I used to play around at song-writing, and I would often use the security of a truck cab to develop my vocal prowess. Some people sing in the shower. I preferred the acoustic camouflage of large industrial engines…partly to protect my good name, but mostly to protect innocent bystanders. So it was, on that fateful day, when Honey Pie and the great steel snake parted company. With fifteen hundred feet of cable singing tight, seven or eight cylinders hammering time, and yours truly belting it out like the reincarnation of Elvis Presley, the shackle pin snapped and all hell broke loose.

It's amazing how quickly your priorities change in a runaway truck. Without warning, Honey Pie let out the mechanical equivalent of a demonic pig squeal, and in what seemed like a split second, I felt my bum-cheeks tighten, called for my mommy and became a born-again Christian. Finally, in a flash of inspiration, I took my foot off the throttle. I stomped on the tractor brakes, but they had no effect. I yanked on the trailer brakes. Ditto. The horn sounded good, but it didn't help either. If the fan had been working, I'm sure I would have ripped it off the dash and held it out the window for wind resistance. It was a stressful thirty seconds.

I was only a few hundred feet from the bottom when the shackle broke, and the last stretch was pretty straight, so when it was all over, me, Honey Pie and fifty tons of cedar were all right-side up. Once the dust settled and the banjo music faded, I peeled myself off the seat, carefully climbed down to dry ground and walked back to check the damage. A quick inspection revealed that with a new shackle and a bit of welding I'd be back in business in no time.

That evening my wild ride and spontaneous religious conversion made for lively conversation around the cookhouse table, but luckily, before I was completely swept away by my newfound sense of sanctimony, Pierre graciously came to my rescue. Prior to becoming a faller, Pierre had spent time studying with members of Montreal's Franciscan order, and in his semi-expert opinion, spiritual transformations in unlicensed vehicles didn't count. In a short mock-ceremony, he waved a spatula over my head and reaffirmed my faith in agnosticism…a blissful uncertainty I enjoy to this day.

Once the hoots and jibes had settled down, it was decided that we would patch up our unorthodox brake system and hope for the best. We were almost out of timber anyway, so the wishful consensus was that Honey Pie had enough left in her tired old frame to finish the claim. You'd think the runaway episode would have been more than enough to remember my logging days by, but as it turned out, Honey Pie had one more trick up her sleeve.

For the next couple weeks things went suspiciously well. The pile in the landing got smaller and smaller, but little by little the gash in the stump got deeper and deeper, and bit by bit the pull got harder and harder. To compensate, the loads got bigger and heavier and bigger and heavier and bigger and heavier. I had run out of gears, and every one of Honey Pie's horses were frothing at the mouth, but I spurred her on, firm in the knowledge that the end of the claim was in sight.

As I walked back one more time to wrestle the eye onto the shackle, I had no way of knowing I was about to change the course of trucking history. (For what it was worth, before climbing back in the cab I checked the brake hoses—force of habit.) As I crested the hill, the snake uncoiled, rose up and snapped to attention. With a sorry-sounding clunk, the slack in Honey's powertrain came tight and the rpm dropped momentarily, but she dug in her heels and we started down. Shiny from wear, the cable coming up the hill matched my speed exactly, but something definitely didn't feel right. When it first started happening, I couldn't quite believe it. As always, a long, low cloud of dust rose from the ditch like smoke from a slow fuse, but ever so gradually, the cable was slowing down. I may not have had a Ph.D. in reactionary physics, but I didn't just fall off the spud wagon either. Instinctively, I knew that if the cable was slowing down it could mean only one thing—so was I! Reverse was out of the question. In a futile attempt to postpone the inevitable, I strained to force the throttle through the floorboards, but there was no getting around it...I was about to stall. Moments later, Honey Pie reached the end of her proverbial rope and *grrrround* to a halt. A sudden and eerie silence settled over the hill. Luckily, I'd already stopped singing.

Alone in a remote wilderness, miles from nowhere and miles from the nearest human being, I climbed to the ground and looked around sheepishly to see if anyone was watching. Somewhere there is an unwritten logger's law, and I had just broken it.

There! I feel much better. Maybe now you can understand why I felt such a need to purge myself. When I'm dead and buried, maybe someone will inscribe the event on my headstone: "Here lies the yutz who stalled a fully loaded, off-highway logging truck while going downhill."

Life goes on, and a few months later I would say goodbye

to logging altogether. I wish I could say it ended on a happy note, but it didn't. After Port Neville I took on a booming contract up near Knight's Inlet. Technically, it was still a gyppo outfit, but compared to Port Neville, this new camp was big-time. The general contractor (we'll call him Cal) had a stump-to-dump contract, brand-new equipment and about fifteen guys. Once the wood hit the water it was my job to ready it for the long tow to the Fraser River. Ruth took a job as second cook. We got along fine with the crew, so for a while it looked like we'd live happily ever after.

When he first stepped on the dock, he seemed like a nice enough guy, and as I helped him tie up his cabin cruiser he asked if I was coming to the union meeting after supper. From the immediacy of his inquiry and the insignia on his boat, it was obvious the man was a union organizer. Like a dummy, I politely explained that even though the camp was unionized, I was self-employed and wasn't actually a member of the crew or the union. With the words "not a member," his whole demeanour began to change. Slowly his lips curled back revealing a sinister set of growing incisors. Long, viscous streams of hot saliva started dripping from his mouth, and as steaming puddles of molten mucus formed at his feet, he leered through his forehead just like Jack Nicholson in *The Shining,* and slowly echoed, "*Not a member?*"

Okay, it wasn't quite that bad, but he did tell me, in no uncertain terms, that if I didn't join the International Woodworkers of America he would make things "uncomfortable" for me with the others…uncomfortable enough that I would either join or leave.

Given the situation, joining the union meant committing financially to an organization that could offer me nothing in return. I'd worked in union camps before and never had any qualms about signing up, but this made no sense. If I didn't like my working conditions I could hardly complain to myself. If I went on strike and couldn't convince myself to meet my wage demands, what was I supposed to do—beat myself up for crossing my own picket line? I can joke about it now, but at the time it wasn't funny at all. Call it what you want, the organizer's threat was extortion, and I fully expected the general contractor to set the guy straight. But to my utter disbelief, when I told Cal what was up, instead of helping me flush the fox out of the bunkhouse, he placed his tail firmly between his legs. His cowardly response is with me to this day. "I don't like it any better than you do," he said, "but it would be better for everyone if you just co-operated." What he really meant was, it would be better for him, and the way I saw it, I had only two choices. I could swallow hard, go with the flow, and keep the first good-money job I'd had in three years, or I could call a plane.

Twenty-four hours later I made my decision. Forty-eight hours later I squeezed Ruth, way too much luggage and eight years of memories into a 185 Cessna and headed for town. It was a gorgeous day, and as we gained altitude, a chaotic tangle of islands and channels fanned out below us like a great unfinished picture puzzle. The flight was like a trip down Memory Lane, and the higher we climbed, the smaller my world seemed to become. At two thousand feet I could retrace the route of the old barge camp that had made it all seem worthwhile. To the west was Donegal Head where Ziggy the sweaty Bavarian gave me my first lesson in fighting stubborn logs. He wore a big thick mackinaw even in the summer, which was kind of weird, but when it came to hang-ups he had a fail-safe system: "If at first you don't succeed, pull like a sonamabitch!" Then there was Blackfish Sound where the camp canine got it in his head one day to follow us all the way to work. It wouldn't have been that unusual if we hadn't gone to work in a boat. Man, that mutt could swim! And off in the misty distance, Alert Bay hadn't changed a bit.

Down below, Havannah Channel was still in the right spot, and over on Vancouver Island, the Adam and Eve Rivers still came together like they were made for each other.

The gyppos are all gone now. In 1983, the tree-farm licence for that whole stretch of coast was handed over to one of the big conglomerates, and one by one the independents were all pushed out. Today, in a little cove on Gilford Island, two old wooden barges are slowly crumbling into the beach. Honey Pie was quite literally put out to pasture. Her bare converted chassis was last seen hauling hay in the Sayward Valley. She's even rumoured to have brakes.

As we passed Ransom Point and the entrance to Port Neville I was seized by an anxious sense of longing. I longed for another time. I longed for another chance. But most of all, I longed for a bag. I don't fly well.

**Sticks and stones
may break my bones,
but ALS is deadly.**

2

D-Day

I t seems like I should be starting this chapter with "It was a dark and stormy night" or something equally ominous, but the truth is, there was nothing ominous about it. In fact it wasn't even night-time, just the start of another normal day. It was March of 1985, and thinking back now, all that really stands out is that I was taking the morning off, something I rarely did. I had just gotten out of the tub and was starting to clip the fingernails of my left hand when I got a really weird twitching feeling between my right thumb and forefinger. My brain was saying squeeze, but nothing was happening. At first I thought there was something wrong with the clippers. I kept waiting to hear that familiar snapping sound, but it never came.

At the time, it didn't seem like the end of the world, but I did find it a little unnerving. After all, the morning before I'd been tossing around cases of dynamite and heavy, steel boom-chains. Why then should a pair of nail-clippers suddenly pose a problem? After several frustrating and fruitless attempts, I put the whole thing down to a touch of tendonitis, and would have left it at that had it not been for Ruth. Out in the kitchen, when I casually mentioned that my hand wasn't working properly, she got quite concerned and insisted I get it checked out. I could say I agreed just to keep peace in the family, but down deep I suppose it was as much for my own peace of mind as hers. Besides, the doctor's office was just up the road, so I threw on a jacket and jumped in the pick-up.

We lived in Kelsey Bay then, a handful of houses midway up the east coast of Vancouver Island. Kelsey still had a store, a fuel dock and the only breakwater for fifty miles. For towboaters, commercial fishermen and guys like myself who hauled marine freight, Kelsey Bay was a good place to wait out a westerly gale, but for outsiders, its real claim to fame was its ferry terminal. Up until a couple of years earlier it had hummed with activity, but when they pushed the highway north to Port Hardy, the ferries pulled out, leaving behind an open patch of blacktop, several aging buildings and a much quieter community. One of these buildings was what we called home.

Technically I was on my way to another town, but Kelsey Bay and the village of Sayward are so close together few people thought of it that way. Nevertheless, even though you could spit from one place to the other, in every way but geographically they were light-years apart. Almost everyone in Sayward worked for the same employer; everyone in Kelsey Bay was self-employed. Sayward's population was stable (about 1,200); Kelsey Bay's numbers quite literally changed with the tide. Sayward was to loggers what Kelsey Bay was to mariners. So a few seconds later, when I pulled into the doctor's driveway and knocked on the door, you could say I had just crossed a kind of cultural divide.

Since setting up his in-home practice a few months earlier, old Doc Meiheutzen had wasted no time providing grist for the rumour mill. I should point out that in loose-lipped little company towns like Sayward, newcomers must pass a rigid set of social requirements. Eccentricities are quickly singled out for lively debate at the local coffee shop, and our new medicine man had already given completely new meaning to the word eccentric. I knocked again.

For reasons known only to himself, and perhaps a few imaginary friends, this greying physician had somehow settled on Sayward as the ideal spot for semi-retirement. His under-the-breath muttering and tinder-dry sense of humour only served to fuel creative but largely inaccurate theories concerning his past. Some folks didn't think he was a doctor at all, believing him instead to be a veteran hit man sent to snuff out key members of the Village Council. Personally, I favoured the experimental head-transplant theory, but I won't go into that here.

I was about to knock a third time when the door finally opened, and the supposedly sinister subject of village speculation greeted me in a well-worn velour housecoat and a wide-eyed pair of puppy-dog slippers. Motioning me to follow, he sleepily led me into his examining room and immediately excused himself to wash and dress. As I waited patiently, I remember thinking his incoherent mutterings meant the mad doctor idea wasn't necessarily that far-fetched, but the sight of those slippers had shot the hit man theory all to hell. No assassin worth his diabolical salt would be caught dead with stuffed cartoon characters on his person. If you're anything like me, you probably like him already.

When the fully dressed Meiheutzen returned, he didn't speak. Instead he studied me quietly as I tried, without success, to twiddle my thumbs. My reason for being there became clear as we both watched my ailing thumb go through a series of sporadic and unnatural jerking movements. I wanted to ask if he had anything for a sick twiddle, but rather than break the silence, I simply held out my hand for his professional opinion. At his command I moved my hand this way and that, clenched my fist once or twice, and then he bonked me a few times with one of those little rubber tomahawks. The examination took barely two minutes (three minutes tops), and before I knew it he had scribbled something on a slip of paper and handed it to me. I half expected to see an illegible prescription for some unpronounceable wonder drug, but instead, all I saw was a neatly printed name and address.

I didn't realize it then, but Meiheutzen's instant reaction to my seemingly minor symptoms hadn't come as a result of haste or indifference. Quite the contrary. Here was a man who had doctored for years in the depths of large metropolitan hospitals. He'd done his time and seen far more than your average country doctor, so the quick decision came from a deep reservoir of practical knowledge. In plain English, Meiheutzen had his shit together.

Suddenly, it was a very different doctor who pulled up a stool and peered at me over his reading glasses. He spoke in a guarded tone, as if choosing his words carefully. The name he'd just given me turned out to be a neuromuscular specialist some distance away in the provincial capital. Ever so gradually, the frank discussion that followed squashed my cocky air of complacency and replaced it with a growing sense of unease. It's hard to remember the whole conversation now, but in the days that followed, four of his words would echo over and over in the back of my mind: "It could be serious."

On the way home, I rehearsed how I would explain what had just transpired without using those four words. I saw no reason to sound the alarm at that point, but somehow, telling Ruth I had to drive two hundred miles for another appointment would have made whichever words I chose seem hollow. You don't put much over on Ruth.

I'd spent the better part of my youth around Victoria, and I still had family within striking distance, so the appointment was a perfect excuse for a visit. I called up my mother and told her to hide the good china. Then we packed up our two pre-schoolers and hit the highway.

A few hours later, in the heart of the Sooke Hills, we pulled up a steep, narrow driveway and came to a stop at the doorstep of a rustic little bungalow. Once the hugs and kisses were spread around, I wandered off with my stepfather, George, to survey their familiar wooded acreage. We leaned up against his truck for a while like guys do. We threw sticks for the dog. Their dog and ours were a lot alike. Both came with a ten-year/twenty-billion-stick warranty. It felt good to be back. When I left home in my late teens, this was the place I had said goodbye to, and enough of my past still lingered to take my mind off why I was there.

Like a lot of mothers, mine had that matronly habit of worrying more about her kids' health than about her own, so I did my best to play down the real reason behind our sudden visit. That evening, after the usual mouth-watering spread of Mom's home cooking, we lay around like fatted calves, played a few hands of cards and caught up on the latest gossip. Despite a late night, sleep was restless and passed much too quickly.

"Diagnosis Day" came with mixed feelings. I hadn't been looking forward to it, but at the same time, I was glad to be getting it over with. After breakfast, Ruth and I drove into the city, found the address and, once inside, took seats in a typically drab waiting area. Almost immediately, a reception-ist ushered us into an examining room and issued instruc-tions to strip to the waist. To break the tension, I made a half-hearted attempt to convince Ruth that the instructions were meant for both of us, but she wouldn't go for it.

When the middle-aged specialist entered the room, he got right down to business. Like Meiheutzen, he made a brief, silent study of the twitching that by this time had spread to my upper arm. Then he had me put my hand through basically the same series of rudimentary movements, and before he could say "I'd rather be golfing," he told me to get dressed and left the room. While he was gone, I came to the conclusion that I was dealing with a truly linear person-ality. Whatever this man lacked in empathy, he more than made up for in insensitivity, and when he returned he wasted no time proving me right. Without the slightest hint of hesi-tation or concern, he took careful aim and dropped his bombshell.

"You have a motor neuron disease called Amyotrophic Lateral Sclerosis." That was what he said, but the way he said it, you would have thought he was diagnosing a twenty-four-hour flu. Nothing in his tone suggested the severity of what he was saying, and as you might expect, my response was one of bewilderment…Amyo what? In the same sterile monotone, he went on to explain that ALS was a progres-sive, untreatable, terminal disorder, and that in all likeli-hood, I'd be dead in under three years.

Perhaps more than anywhere else, this is where I wanted to offer something profound, but the truth is, I can't think of an eloquent description for numbness. How does one describe, with any feeling, the absence of feeling? There was no sense of loss—no audible gasp or display of emotion—only numb-ness. His matter-of-fact manner took me completely off guard, and when Ruth and I first looked at one another, I'm not sure either of us thought he was serious, but we soon would. The office was right across the street from Victoria's Jubilee Hospital, and when we heard him phone over to request a bed and a test for Mr. Kaye, reality began to sink in.

It was all happening too fast. The day had started with family in the warmth of hearth and home, and was ending with three grizzled-up geezers in the sanitary chill of an acute-care ward. One of my roommates had just undergone cataract surgery and spent the entire night carrying on a drug-induced conversation with his bedside table. Luckily, the stroke victim right next to me was securely strapped to the rails of his bed. Each time I dared to nod off, he'd thrash around like a drunken sailor and yell obscenities at me. The third guy just lay there with his eyes half closed and his mouth wide open. He never moved, never spoke, and as close as I could tell, never breathed as long as I was there. The nurse assured me he was alive, but I still have my doubts. It wasn't a good night.

The following morning I had to forego breakfast, and by nine o'clock I was prepped and ready for a spinal myelogram. I understand the procedure has improved dramatically since I had mine—a non-toxic dye, used in Great Britain for twelve years prior, was finally introduced here in 1986—but in the early eighties, myelograms, if performed improperly, ranked right up there with Chinese water torture. If you've never had the pleasure, a basic description goes something like this. Once a local anesthetic takes effect, a large syringe is used to puncture the base of the spine. Spinal fluid is then drawn off, and a similar amount of radio opaque solution (dye) is injected. With the aid of an oscillating table, the patient is tipped this way and that, causing the dye to flow in a predictable fashion. By tracking the dye's movement and monitoring its flow rate, an experienced eye can detect abnormal pressure points along the spinal cord. Unfortunately, although great care is usually taken, it isn't uncommon for patients to tip beyond the critical angle at which dye reaches the brain. Because the dye is itself a recognized toxin, when this happens, problems can arise. In my case, problems arose.

For the next twelve hours I was overtaken with heaving nausea, violent headache and something midway between sleep and delirium. Call me paranoid, but whenever I looked at the man who didn't breathe, he'd use ventriloquism to taunt me. His lips never moved, but a couple times I could've sworn I heard the Captain and Tenille singing "Muskrat Love" at seventy-eight speed. At the peak of my reaction, I pleaded with the nurse for some of the stuff that made you talk to the furniture, but for reasons known only to her, and other like-minded sadists, she wasn't allowed to administer any thing for my discomfort.

It's kind of foggy now, but sometime in the midst of all this medically inflicted misery, Mr. Personality dropped in long enough to tell me the myelogram hadn't turned up anything to change his original diagnosis, and that once my head cleared, I was free to go. Then he basically told me to have a nice death, and left.

Never before, and never since, have I met a more pathetic excuse for a doctor. He may have had the dextrous skill of an accredited neurosurgeon and academic credentials coming out his Hippocratic ying-yang, but when it came to the relative simplicity of verbal communication, he was a rank amateur. In years to come, I'd have the pleasure of meeting many, more amiable members of the medical community, and fortunately, one of them would come to the fore before we left town.

In between heaves, I'd already decided to seek a second opinion, and I wasted no time doing just that. Still a little shaky but moving under my own steam, I released myself from hospital and headed across town with Ruth to the recuperative sanctuary of my sister's couch. Glenna's townhouse, on the outskirts of Victoria, was just the right size for a single, working mother of two, but whenever we came on the scene it got downright cosy. The racket that erupts when two young families like ours get together can be trying, but this time, the noise became a welcome distraction. In all the excitement, I could hardly hear my future caving in around me.

First thing the following morning, Ruth and I went through the Yellow Pages, found the physician section and scanned for anything with a neuromuscular handle attached to it. Using the "close your eyes and point" method, we eventually settled on a nice, solid-sounding name, Dr. Charles Simpson. Over the phone, a polite receptionist informed me that in order to see Dr. Simpson, or any specialist for that matter, I'd need yet another referral.

No problem. I'm a reasonable man. After all, what was one more minor runaround between friends? It's not like it was a matter of life or death or anything. All I had to do was phone my sister at work. She, in turn, would phone her family doctor and ask for an appointment. He, in turn, would phone the specialist and ask for an appointment. I, in turn, would get a more favourable diagnosis, and all would be right with the world. No problem!

Glenna's doctor came to the rescue by squeezing me in as soon as we got there. He'd never seen anyone with ALS before, and admitted he didn't know anything about it, but he could dial a telephone just like an old pro. How much this kind of inter-office back-scratching costs the taxpayer each year is open for debate, but at that moment, who cared? All I could hear was the sound of my own emotional ice cracking, and I was glad to be getting one step closer to solid ground.

Dr. Simpson graciously agreed to set aside a few minutes of his lunch break, so we raced back into the city. A few minutes turned into an hour and a half of questions from us, questions from him, and a lot of non-answers all around. Aside from hearing that my demise would likely come as a result of respiratory failure, I didn't learn much. Knowledge of ALS is so limited, I won't bother elaborating on the details of our discussion, except to say that Charles Simpson was everything the other specialist wasn't. His diagnosis was exactly the same, but for what it was worth, this time it came with a feeling of resolution.

If I compare that first specialist to a magistrate, and his examination to a preliminary hearing, then by getting a second opinion you could say I had exhausted my final appeal. The verdict was in, and a sentence had been handed down…Death by Suffocation.

Before we left for Kelsey Bay, Mom filled a big bag with enough homemade goodies to feed a small army, but by that time I'd lost my appetite. Usually I enjoyed the scenic drive up Vancouver Island, but the trip home seemed to take way longer than it should have. Passing scenery became a tedious blur. Songs on the radio all sounded depressing and distant. My hands stayed on the wheel, and my eyes stayed on the road, but I wasn't in control.

Looking back now, I probably shouldn't have been driving, but if it makes any sense, it felt good to be putting miles between me and the whole indecipherable mess. No known cause. No known treatment. No known cure. Aside from a new-found notion of my own mortality, all I could say I had learned for sure was that I was fasciculating. You and I call them twitches. To doctors they're fasciculations. Call them what you want, mine were still spreading, and by the time we made it home, that feeling of resolution was fading fast.

This will sound phony to some
but, for a time, the red tape
surrounding my diagnosis
made dying seem like
the least of my worries.

3

The Big Lie

Is life really a Mutual affair? How about McDonald's...do they really do it all for us? Nobody takes corporate slogans very seriously, but what you may find frightening is that the claims of our so-called social safety nets are every bit as bogus. If I sound cynical, it's with good reason. If I sound bitter, it's because I am.

You don't have to be a psychology major to appreciate the frame of mind that follows a terminal diagnosis. For the first few days, I kept slipping in and out of character like some kind of an emotional chameleon. On the outside I'm pretty sure I never flinched, but on the inside I hovered precariously between the protective sanctuary of denial and the seductive appeal of all-out panic. Denial would eventually win the day, but luckily, for a critical period in the beginning, an inner voice kept saying over and over, "Get your affairs in order." On the surface it sounded easy enough, but as it turned out, what lay ahead would be anything but easy. What lay ahead was a highly organized and near-impenetrable infrastructure of bureaucratic buck-passing and institutional indifference, an infrastructure designed to systematically shunt me ever closer to the welfare wicket.

But before you label me as just another angry invalid, I need to take you back a year or so. In those days we were leasing an old homestead in the Sayward Valley, and I was doing a bit of hobby farming on the side. No big deal—half a dozen cows, a pen full of pigs, some free-range chickens, two ducks, an old grey mare named Birdy and just enough cats to keep both our dogs busy. It was an idyllic setting on the banks of the Salmon River, seventeen acres of lush pastureland right at the foot of a snow-peaked Mount H'Kusam. By yuppie standards, the two-storey farmhouse was rundown and shabby, but compared to my gyppo logging years, it was pretty uptown.

On this particular morning, Ruth and I sat together at our dining-room table. Seated across from us was an insurance salesman, and the three of us were weighing the obvious dangers of my job against the marginal cost of life insurance. I considered myself a cautious skipper, but I made my living on the Johnstone and Queen Charlotte Straits, neither of which has ever been known for predictable weather. And admittedly, I did spend long periods working alone loading haywire equipment in the middle of nowhere, in the middle of gales, often in the middle of the night. Couple all this with the Coast Guard's periodic use of me as an auxiliary rescue service, and in the salesman's words, I was a "prime candidate." I'm also a pretty easy sell, so after a short, low-key sales pitch, I signed on the dotted line.

I only mention this insurance episode to underscore my feeling of having at least some of my "affairs in order." The policy I chose not only covered my death but included a disability waiver as well. In my own mind I was invincible, but for an extra eight bucks a month, Ruth got to sleep a bit easier. In retrospect, adding that little bit extra turned out to be the smartest thing I've ever done. Who would have thought that barely a year later we'd be scrambling to read the fine print. The waiver stated that if I became unable to work, we'd get a thousand dollars per month until the day I died; not enough for caviar, but nobody would go hungry either.

Without getting too technical, my situation fit the bill. The way it was explained to me, through normal activity, our muscles are in an ongoing state of destruction and reconstruction. ALS allows the destruction part to continue but gradually destroys our ability to rebuild, so my body had become a non-renewable resource...something to be preserved at all costs. My job on the freight boat, and the strenuous activity that went with it, was now much more than a detriment to my health—it was life-threatening!

Once I got over the initial shock of D-Day, I broke the news to the salesman, the wheels were put in motion, and an obligatory waiting period began. Next, I had to explain to my father that the time had come for him to step back into harness. In theory, we were already partners in the freight business, but to that point he hadn't had to spend much time around the work end of things. Our unexpected role reversal didn't come easy for either of us. Dad was a hustler by nature. His home was his office and he usually answered his phone on the first ring. But for me, hanging around the house was truly an alien concept. Houses are nice enough places to visit, but I never expected to have to live in one.

For the first week or so, my pacing just about drove Ruth nuts. In her words, I was like a caged animal, and my keen jungle senses told me that unless I wanted to join the list of endangered species I'd better steer clear of the kitchen. I wanted to live long enough to die young, so I voluntarily banished myself to the basement for some heavy-duty brooding.

For a little while I actually enjoyed looking out across the freight yard with coffee in hand. Dad would eventually make the transition, but the first few months were pretty hard on him. He was over fifty, smoked like a chimney and had a weak back, so he hired a couple gofers to run around, lift heavy objects and handle the dirty stuff. I hate to admit it, but watching three men struggle to do what I'd always been expected to do by myself gave me a glib sense of satisfaction. The novelty wore off quickly, though, and before long, satisfaction turned to frustration.

If the reason for my sudden abundance of idle time had been something pleasant, I could have spent it doing something pleasant, but no...I had to go all cerebral. I had to take stock of my life like some kind of new-age sensitive guy. Forming a sort of mental balance sheet, I began weighing the things I'd always wanted to do against the few things I'd actually done, and no matter how I tabulated the results, the bottom line was the same. Almost all my accomplishments were in one way or another connected, not to *my* aspirations, but to the aspirations of my father. I don't want this to turn into an Oprah-style confession, but from the time I was a kid working my summer holidays, I'd been helping my father meet his goals and obligations. Except for a couple of years in my late teens, I'd spent the past fourteen years meeting someone else's deadlines. It was nothing to be ashamed of. Lots of sons try to help out their dads, but suddenly, in the blink of an eye, I found myself pushing thirty and facing a deadline of my own...the ultimate deadline.

After a couple of days of basement brainstorming, I was left with two options. To subsidize our income, I'd either have to find a less strenuous career (very quickly) or start liquidating my assets. Option number two would have been infinitely more plausible if it weren't for one key factor…I didn't have any assets. Aside from a second-hand Chev pickup and a couple of rooms' worth of well-worn furniture, I had absolutely nothing of value to show for my efforts.

When it came right down to it, my only ace in the hole seemed to be my ability with a camera. During my years of coastal cruising, I had put together a pretty decent collection of images, many of which had sold for respectable sums in the past. I'd never had time to pursue it full-time, but if I was supposed to avoid strenuous activities, then photography was just what the doctor ordered. I already had a few prints, I already had a few frames, and I already had a portfolio. All I really needed to get the ball rolling was a small loan to market my handiwork…or so I thought. (I'd eventually turn to video and form my own production company, but that's another book.)

For months my bank had been sending me sappy letters telling me what a great guy I was. "If you're planning a vacation, don't hesitate to call us, Mr. Kaye." "Isn't it time for a new vehicle, Mr. Kaye?" "You're number one with us, Mr. Kaye." I should point out that for sixteen years I'd been borrowing from, and making payments to, the same bank, and that during those sixteen years I had never (repeat) never missed a payment. So when I drove the fifty miles to Campbell River and strolled in to see my friendly banker, the thought of rejection was the furthest thing from my mind. In the brief meeting that followed, I found out exactly how much my patronage was valued.

The stumbling block came midway down their application form, on a line that read: "Please State Current Income." How could I? That was my reason for being there. I had become a liability, and suddenly, thanks to ALS, my spotless credit rating wasn't even worth a two thousand dollar personal loan.

Thanks to ALS, for the first time I'd hear the four words I would come to loathe. "I'm sorry, Mr. Kaye."

When I think back now, I'm both ashamed and embarrassed by my childish naivety. I actually believed the commercials. You know the ones. Using a variety of warm family images, and a lot of soft focus, our banking institutions try to convince us how they'll be there to lend a hand when we need them most. The truth is, when the chips are down, our reputations are only as good as our last paycheque.

Feeling rejected and betrayed, I left the bank and headed for my next nemesis, the Campbell River office of the Unemployment Insurance Commission. I don't know what it is about government offices, but I always seem to enter them under full sail and exit feeling like I've just escaped some sort of civilian-sucking doldrum.

I should point out that, aside from a couple months of benefits a decade before, handouts had never been part of my M.O. Maybe being self-employed distorts one's view of civil servants, but I swear some of them even think in triplicate. I took a number and joined a line of ten or twelve people. The funniest things cross your mind in a UIC lineup. I checked the time on their big round government-issue wall clock. I counted fuzzballs on the guy in front of me. I timed my pulse against the big round government-issue wall clock. I checked for fuzzballs on myself. Every so often, the line would heave a collective sigh and quietly shuffle forward a few inches. I'd heard awful stories of people disappearing in these lineups, never to be seen or heard from again, and I remember wanting desperately to break the stifling silence: "Uh, excuse me, but I don't have long to live."

Just as I started thinking my number might come up before my number came up, my number came up. I stepped up to the counter, brushed the cobwebs aside and was confronted by a decidedly snotty, middle-aged woman.

"Confronted" and "snotty" may seem a bit harsh, but it's definitely the most accurate way to describe her manner of greeting people. Her mouth said, "Can I help you?" but her tone of voice said, "No matter how long the line gets, or how rudely I treat you, I don't stand a chance in hell of ever being fired, but hey, I could help you if I really wanted to." I knew prolonged eye contact with this kind of person could result in acute oxygen deprivation, but I was a man on a mission, and no risk was too great. Throwing pride and caution to the wind, I looked her squarely in the eyes and made my case for assistance.

After hearing the condensed version of my situation, a flicker of empathy came across her face, and for a moment she seemed to forget her poor, miserable existence. Then she ushered me to a little cubicle near the back and turned me over to an employment counsellor. Unlike the receptionist, the counsellor's friendly tone put me at ease right away, but unfortunately, after hearing my story, the sense of ease was quickly replaced with disappointment.

As she spoke, it was easy to tell she'd been forced to make the same speech a thousand times before. In her calm, practised way, she pointed out that, due to my admission of unemployability, I would only get a partial allowance for a period of sixteen weeks...after that I'd be on my own. "I'm sorry, Mr. Kaye."

Finding a cure for ALS in the next couple of months didn't seem likely, so as I left the building I'd already written off UIC as my second strike of the day. The drive back to Kelsey Bay gave me lots of time to reflect on the day's failures, and by the time I stopped in Sayward to grab our mail, I was a pretty unhappy camper. Waiting in our post office box was an official-looking notice from Canada Pension that could only be described as strike three. With the words of the banker and counsellor still ringing in my ears, the letter started with (what else) "I'm sorry, Mr. Kaye, but after carefully reviewing your application, blah, blah, blah." It went on to say, in that warm federal way, that pursuant to current guidelines, my present state of deterioration was incompatible with eligibility. It wasn't all bad, though. I may have been disqualified from disability benefits, but in a roundabout way, they made it clear I could always reapply when I started gasping for air.

I can't remember if I even greeted Ruth when I got home. By this time my status as the great white breadwinner was pretty much shattered, so I more than likely just took up my post in the basement and continued pacing. For a while, with the help of the Provincial Ombudsman, I even made an appeal to the Workers Compensation Board, but they too turned a deaf ear.

I was beginning to understand why our social institutions refer to themselves as safety nets; by definition, they're full of holes! It's always darkest before the dawn, though, and in the proverbial nick of time, we got our first glimmer of financial hope. It came in the form of our first insurance cheque, and for a little while the wolves were kept at bay.

Having a monthly security blanket, however minimal, can alleviate a certain amount of societal pressure, but in my case, the cheques did absolutely nothing to curb a dwindling sense of self-worth. Instead, each time I looked in the mirror, my seemingly healthy reflection only reinforced a growing sense of inadequacy. You must remember that at that time, nothing in my stature suggested I should need help of any kind...financial or otherwise. For all intents and purposes I was an outwardly healthy young man.

The chain of events that follows brought out a side of me that had, to that point, lain hidden, even to me. And although it may seem like I'm digressing, if you're ever to understand the rationale behind my subsequent behaviour, you must also understand the underlying part of my nature that I was suppressing at the time.

One seldom sees words like "deadbeat" or "lazy" used in the same sentence with ALS. In fact, one of the only traits ALSers seem to share is an energetic past. In almost every case, victims are either classic over-achievers or chronic workaholics. Now, both these types live lives that revolve around work, but their motivations are different, so it's important that you understand which side of the fence I fall on.

I've been called a workaholic, and I suppose if the work-boot fits…but technically, even though I worked all the time, I was never driven by an addiction to work so much as an aversion to, perhaps even a disdain for, boredom.

The way I see it, over-achievers set goals and pursue those goals to the exclusion of all else. The sad part is, achievement rarely begets satisfaction, only the setting of new goals.

Workaholics, on the other hand, are quite satisfied typing letters one day and digging ditches the next. They think nothing of changing goals in midstream and rarely, if ever, achieve anything of consequence.

This must be starting to sound like I'm introducing myself at an AA meeting—"Hi, my name is Dennis and I have a working problem." The point I'm having such a hard time making is this: the workaholic me is gradually disappearing and an over-achieving me is beginning to emerge. In more tangible terms, writing a book is a perfect example of the personal metamorphosis a disease like ALS can put someone through. It simply isn't something the old Dennis would have taken on…started maybe, but finished? Never.

Now, compare where I was then to where I am now, and perhaps you can appreciate that it was a very different Dennis who was pacing the floor in Kelsey Bay. We only had one channel, so the TV quickly lost its appeal. I've never been one for soap operas anyway, and I already knew most of the stuff on "Sesame Street," so it was no great loss. I might have even taken up knitting if I'd been *reeeally* fast with one hand. But after a while, even the most dedicated pacer has to find an outlet for his surplus energy. I was quickly approaching meltdown when, like manna from heaven, the timely solution to all my problems came.

As luck would have it, back in Campbell River, a handful of gutsy young entrepreneurs were just getting a brand-new cottage brewery off the ground. I desperately needed something to keep me busy, and they desperately needed help. It didn't matter how you looked at it; we were made for each other.

I was an experienced skipper — they needed a marketing director.
I really needed money — they didn't have any.
I liked beer — they had beer.

Almost overnight I went from well-worn greasy blue jeans and Stanfield woollies to well-washed dress slacks and colour-co-ordinated sweater vests…from navigating some of the fastest salt-water rapids on earth to espousing the virtues of naturally aged beer. It took some adjustment. Not everyone is cut out to spend hours on end in smoke-filled bars, surrounded by loud talk, laughter and buckets of free joy-juice, but I knew I was up to the challenge.

All sarcasm aside, like most fledgeling businesses, this group was seriously under-financed and couldn't have paid me even if they'd wanted to. This suited me just fine. If you've ever tried lifting a beer keg with one hand, you'll know I couldn't do much without help anyway. On days when I wasn't emotionally fit enough to play the salesman, I felt no obligation to perform. I came and went as I pleased, so when I didn't feel up to it, I'd just disappear for a while and reappear when I was back on top of my game. I couldn't in all honesty say I had a job, but it kept my mind off things and gave me the marginal satisfaction of feeling useful.

The beer was a cinch to sell everywhere but in its own hometown, and without preservatives, the lack of turnover with the locals became the company's downfall. Once the product started going downhill, the little brewery never stood a chance, but at a time when I needed support, it was a great place to be, and the staff was like a second family.

What looked on the surface to be smooth sailing quickly turned out to be the calm before the storm. No sooner had the insurance cheques started coming than I began getting the insurance company's annoying medical questionnaires. They were a pain in the ass, but I considered them a necessary evil. The procedure was always the same: give the questionnaire to my doctor, he'd check me over, reaffirm the disease's progress, sign it and send it back. For reasons I still don't fully understand, on one of these questionnaires my doctor took it upon himself to mention my affiliation with the brewery, and in his ignorance he mistakenly classified it as gainful employment.

Needless to say, the insurance company smelled blood and went straight for the jugular. Their next correspondence wasn't a questionnaire. Instead, they blindsided me with a notice of severance, and the next thing I knew, I was right back in the same financial quagmire. "I'm sorry, Mr. Kaye."

What followed was nothing less than a heartless and calculated display of corporate stonewalling. First I tried to contact the original salesman, but he wouldn't return my calls. Then, in letters to head office, I politely tried to explain how they had based their severance on an unfortunate misunderstanding. They responded with letters politely telling me to get lost. Next, in letters of protest, I tried the not-so-polite approach, categorically rejecting their decision. They responded with not-so-polite letters, rejecting my rejections...and the file grew.

It was truly a time of firsts. For the first time in my life, I had absolutely no income on the horizon. For the first time in my life, bills were piling up. And for the first time in my life, I found myself seeking the advice of a lawyer. Oddly enough, it was the latter that really had my feathers ruffled. In my estimation, lawyers had always fit somewhere between civil servants and the bottom of the food chain, so just making the appointment left a sour taste in my mouth. It was one of two myths that would fall by the wayside that day. On principle, using a shark to keep sharks away struck me as an admission of weakness, but surprisingly, that first encounter would forever change my opinion of lawyers and the role at least some of them play.

After listening carefully to my story, he excused himself momentarily, and when he returned I got the thumbs-up. Presumably, he went to consult his colleagues, but he might have just gone to the can or something. At any rate, his law firm had a special fund to cover charity cases just like mine, and he assured me his services wouldn't cost me a cent. He was confident the insurance company would come around to my way of thinking, but there was a downside. In his words, it was going to take some time, and in the interim, I'd have to make do on social assistance.

Who, me? I wasn't a low-life bum. Only low-life bums went on welfare. Right? If making an appointment with a lawyer left a sour taste in my mouth, then the thought of going on social assistance made me want to gag. Campbell River's welfare office was only three blocks away, so I'd barely gotten over the shock of meeting a warm-blooded lawyer when I came face to face with the day's second misconception: the cold-blooded civil servant.

When I pulled up in front of the building, I carefully

scanned the parking lot for anyone I knew, anyone I didn't know but might know me, and anyone who didn't know me but might know someone I knew. The coast was clear. In a vain attempt to suck my entire body up behind my sunglasses, I took a deep breath and made a break for the entrance. I already had an image in my head of what it would be like, and to begin with, everything fit—another drab waiting room, a few personal-affirmation posters. I whispered my name to the woman behind the counter, quietly expressed my wish to see a social worker and took a seat.

So it had come down to this. I felt like a duck out of water—like Arlo Guthrie on the bench marked group "W." None of the information pamphlets that were scattered around seemed to be meant for me. I'd never done time, wasn't pregnant and, despite a checkered past, didn't require methadone treatment. Nobody had bothered to write a pamphlet for the terminally ill workaholic with deep-seated phobias about government handouts.

When the moment of truth came, you'd have thought I was being called to my execution. I was led down a narrow hallway to a small, windowless office and introduced to my executioner…another woman. I probably would have noticed her soft smile, bottomless eyes and knockout body, but I was a family man, so rather than ogle, I crawled out from behind my sunglasses and took my best shot at grovelling. Apprehension must have been written all over my face, because from the second I sat down the social worker seemed to go out of her way to justify my being there. By the end of our conversation, my guilt complex was history, and by the time I left the building we had struck a face-saving deal where I would reimburse the ministry, if and when my lawyer won a retroactive settlement.

For the next few months it was out of my hands. My lawyer and the insurance lawyers fired their legal arrows back and forth, I collected welfare, and the file grew. In a last-ditch attempt to dodge their responsibility, the insurance company started sending the same questionnaires again, this time, directing me to be reexamined by far-away specialists of their choosing.

Finally, just days before a court action would have ensued, we received a letter of reinstatement and retroactive payment in full. Obviously, the motive behind their questionnaires had never been to gain information; it was to tire me of providing it!

In summary, the breakdown goes like this:

My Bank—wouldn't help because I wasn't working.
Unemployment Insurance Commission—wouldn't help because I wasn't fit enough to work.
Canada Pension—wouldn't help because I wasn't unfit enough not to work.
Workers Compensation Board—wouldn't help because I couldn't prove work was involved.
Private Insurance—wouldn't help because I dared to attempt work.

It would be a year before Canada Pension would have a similar change of heart, but for now, there were a few valuable lessons to be learned from this sorry chain of events. Not all lawyers are overpaid, not all bureaucrats are underqualified, and not all welfare bums are welfare bums. And perhaps the most important lesson of all...cover your ass! If you think that you and yours are in good hands, think again! These days you need a lot of energy if you want to be sick.

In all, it had been nine meagre and worrisome months since joining the ranks of the financially destitute, and with the resumption of insurance cheques came an entirely new attitude. What started out making me feel guilty has become a monthly source of sweet revenge. The longer I live, the better it feels. I paid one more visit to Social Services, paid my debt to society and paid a silent compliment to one very civil civil servant. This time I wasn't wearing sunglasses.

It's been said that the primary difference

between doctors and God

is that God doesn't think

he's a doctor.

4

Doctors and Other Deities

Prior to my diagnosis I'd spent my days, nights, weekends and holidays skippering a custom-built landing craft called the *Joint Venture* up and down the B.C. coast. The vessel was powered by two Mercedes-Benz industrial engines, each one generating just shy of a thousand horsepower. On paper, this sixty-foot aluminum vessel should have gone fast enough to leave ideas behind, but from the day it was launched, its unorthodox and inferior design rendered it incapable of speeds over ten knots. Unfortunately, none of this made a whit of difference to our banker; one way or another, he would have his pound of flesh. So I traded in my racing gloves for steel-toed rubbers and a sou'wester, rolled up my sleeves and went to work.

Over the course of six years I carried everything from baby ducks to powder trucks. In summer I shuffled around fire-fighting equipment. Fall and winter brought forestry crews with their four-by-fours and spacing gear. And every spring, millions and millions of young trees. Destinations ranged from salmon hatcheries to remote Indian villages, even the odd prospecting claim. But on the majority of runs I carried boom-gear, explosives and rolling stock to wilderness logging camps. Working the tides meant being on call around the clock, and because the boat was so slow, the hours were notoriously long. (My record was 43 hours on 3 hours sleep.)

Along with its less than impressive speed, the *Joint Venture*'s unusual design also created an unavoidable airfoil. This meant that as I lumbered along from place to place, a persistent cloud of diesel smoke re-circulated around and through the cabin and wheelhouse. With a couple thousand horsepower and twenty-four cylinders hammering away, a substantial amount of exhaust is generated, to say the least. Combine all this with a faulty inboard exhaust system, and it goes without saying that inhalation of diesel exhaust became part of my daily diet.

Aside from a slight eye irritation and an unpleasant odour, I felt no ill effects. Conversely, when customers chose to travel with their freight, complaints ranged from "This is gross!" to claims of dizziness, headache and nausea. Some would adamantly refuse to ride inside the wheelhouse, choosing instead to ride in the shelter of one of the vehicles on deck. On extreme days, if no shelter could be found, the hardy ones simply opted to stand outside and brave the weather. Understandably, the boat's local reputation as somewhat of an engineering albatross grew, but work kept coming in, so I kept going out.

Then came ALS. Words like "freight" and "muscle" belong

together, and for good reason. ALS turns muscle from something we take for granted to something only a fool would waste. Physical exercise becomes an exercise in futility, so with my diagnosis came my final trip.

For financial reasons, deck hands had almost always been an unaffordable luxury, and so with the exception of one very brief period, my years at the wheel were spent alone. When I tied up the *Joint Venture* for the last time, the ship's log revealed that individual engine hours stood at just over six thousand, and five thousand eight hundred of those hours were mine. Consequently, somewhere deep within the recesses of my layman's brain, I concluded that living in a toxic cloud for several thousand hours might somehow be linked to my condition.

I'd seen television reports stating that, like gasoline, diesel fuel contained a variety of toxins, including lead and other heavy metals. But when I presented the lead/ALS scenario to my specialists, they dismissed the allegation as medically groundless. To my dismay, such a connection proved too great a stretch for the expert trio who would ultimately share in my diagnosis.

Specialist # 1 (Mr. Personality) had all the bedside manner of an impeccably dressed mannequin.

Prognosis: You have ALS.
There is no cure.
No one knows what causes ALS.
It can't be what you think it is.

Specialist #2 (Dr. Charles Simpson) was like a breath of fresh air, taking pains to at least tackle my questions. His understanding manner went a long way toward bursting the

bubble of stress, animosity and fear so expertly crafted by
Specialist #1.

Prognosis: You have ALS.
 There is no cure.
 No one knows what causes ALS.
 It can't be what you think it is.

Specialist #3 (Dr. Andrew Eisen) seemed inquisitive,
professionally courteous, willing to answer questions, was
recognized as western Canada's top dog and came highly
recommended by Specialist #2.

Prognosis: You have ALS.
 There is no cure.
 No one knows what causes ALS.
 It can't be what you think it is.

When a man, for whatever reason, is suddenly pulled from
the wilds of British Columbia's north coast, then dropped
into the high-tech world of twentieth century medicine, a
certain degree of awe and intellectual submission takes place.
I'm not ashamed to say that when the reason for the abrupt
transition is an incurable and terminal illness (especially one
you've never heard of), that feeling of submission knows no
bounds. When individuals infinitely more educated than
yourself tell you there's no connection whatsoever between
your symptoms and the inhalation of diesel exhaust, you gaze
up through the stratosphere at your all-knowing healers and
think to yourself, "Yeah, right." I may have been over-
whelmed, but I wasn't stupid.

The story would have ended there had it not been for a
new-found friend named David Zamluk. An accountant,
with no medical background, David developed a keen interest in my suspicions and took it upon himself to research

the chemical make-up of diesel exhaust, along with several case histories of lead poisoning. He was forever shoving old medical texts under my nose that not only documented neuromuscular complications in cases of lead poisoning but stressed the imperative need for early detection. David repeatedly urged me to help him present his findings to my specialists, but being in the first stages of denial, I saw no legitimate reason to press the issue, and, initially at least, I resisted his advice. After all, if you aren't really sick, why bother making waves?

Cutting to the chase, I eventually agreed and made an appointment with my family doctor. David put his lunch hour aside, and before I knew it, we were thumbing through magazines in the large waiting room of Campbell River's Alder Medical Clinic. The Alder Clinic is one of those modern places shared by a dozen or more doctors. Its bright, colour-coded decor is, I suppose, a visual attempt to put children at ease. Were it not for starch-white nurses flitting in and out of colour-coded doors with colour-coded files under their arms, one could easily have mistaken the place for a day-care centre or elementary school. So when the head starch-white called out my name, it seemed as though I were being summoned to the principal's office. She guided us to the usual door and I entered first. My doctor greeted me with a smile, but as David entered close behind, the smile vanished and was quickly replaced by a look I can only describe as half panic, half contempt. Even before speaking, I realized that by bringing a stranger unannounced, I had unknowingly breached some ancient doctor-patient code of ethics, and that David's mere presence was enough to open a sore for which the good doctor had no cure. Right before my very eyes, the Jekyll I thought I knew displayed an unpredictable and ultra-defensive alter-ego. Even as I reiterated David's findings, I could hear my words rebounding off an impenetrable Hyde. The doctor I knew had a gentle manner and an understanding personality, but on this day I saw a side of him that I've come to learn is, with the exception of a few individuals, characteristic of his entire profession. (I say, "with the exception of a few individuals" because the doctor I have now drives an old pick-up, makes house calls and has an incurably therapeutic sense of humour. I also have an out-of-town specialist who doesn't have an insecure bone in her body.)

In the doctor's defence, it's only fair to say that David, being an accountant on his lunch break, was dressed in the usual accountant type garb: dress shoes, dark pants, white shirt and tie. It's possible that one could have mistaken him for another G.P., or worse yet, a lawyer. Perhaps his white-collar persona was enough to set off some cross-profession rivalry unknown in my limited gumboot circles.

At any rate, Doc made no attempt to hide his disdain, and so, for the entire meeting, a tight, uncomfortable atmosphere prevailed. The meeting was short. On leaving, aside from a brief acknowledgment of the meeting's failure, neither David nor I found it necessary to expand on what had just taken place. It was all too clear that to seek an answer outside the halls of conventional medical knowledge was to tread on sacred ground. In doing so, I had come upon a sort of Tarzan mentality. The unwritten law in this new jungle was "Me doctor—you patient," and being taken seriously would require a more gentle approach, one not so apt to rile the natives.

That first meeting had been such a disaster that when David suggested we combine his next business trip to the capital with a visit to my Victoria specialist, I was willing to tag along but didn't share Dave's optimism at all. I wasn't about to make the same mistake twice, so I made a point of calling ahead.

A few days later, there we were, sitting in the small but tastefully decorated waiting room of Specialist #2. Over the phone I had made it very clear that I would be accompanied by someone who might be wearing a tie, but that we would be coming in peace. So when we entered the examining room, a smile and friendly greeting was extended to us both. However, despite the smile and the conversation's amiable tone, you still could have cut the air with a scalpel. Try as we might, our efforts to appear nonthreatening had no effect, and try as he might, Specialist #2 was unable to relax his defensive posture.

Where our diplomacy, a few days earlier, had been scorched by professional indifference, we now found ourselves drowning in professional patronizing. My specialist assured me he understood my concern but implied that mine was not to reason why…mine was but to go and die. This comparatively mellow rebuff was more subtle than the first, but was equally effective.

Apart from the dated material that David had, I had neither the training nor the practical knowledge to argue any medical case, let alone one that has dumbfounded researchers for more than a century. What I did have, though, was an intuitive sense that a hundred-plus years of fruitless research had left doctors feeling just a wee bit testy. Simply being there was not, in itself, intimidating. More to the point, the perceived threat lay in my basic premise: I was daring to attach importance to information that my doctors ruled unimportant. I began to theorize that investigation or self-analysis of any kind was, in their eyes, a direct challenge to their academic prowess.

Proof for my theory came a few weeks later when, under similar circumstances, we called on Specialist #3. In terms of neuromuscular expertise, my Vancouver specialist was British Columbia's high priest, so extra pains were taken to keep him on side. This time, after the usual pleasantries, I reported my most recent symptoms, intentionally delaying any mention of lead or heavy metals. As long as we discussed what ALS "had done" to me, what ALS "was doing" to me, or what ALS "would do" to me, the lines of communication remained open, but the instant I presented my assertion of "why" I might have ALS, dialogue switched to dial tone. We were still in the same room, but it was as if we'd been talking on the phone and the line had suddenly gone dead.

It was now painfully obvious that any analysis on my part was doomed to fall on deaf ears. Despite the doctor's evasive stance, however, our persistence didn't go entirely unrewarded. It was agreed that my tender age alone (uncharacteristically young for ALS) was enough to open a tiny window of diagnostic doubt. A battery of tests was ordered, and a few weeks later I was admitted to Vancouver General Hospital. I was freeze-dried, deep-fried, blood-tested and medically molested for six days—electromyography, positron emission tomography, magnetic resonance imaging, nuclear magnetic resonance, computerized axial tomography, electrocardiogram, electroencephalogram—you name it, I got it. Under normal circumstances I wouldn't have minded having my image resonated, and if I thought for a minute it would do any good they could have computerized my axial till the cows came home, but after a while I got the impression that the entire exercise was nothing more than a high-tech attempt to pacify me. The experience may have been doing wonders for my vocabulary, but notably absent were any tests for metal poisoning.

As luck would have it, during my stay in Vancouver I was invited to dine at a group home for the physically disabled. During dinner, one of the residents asked why I was undergoing tests. I reiterated the now familiar story of my diagnosis and the refusal of doctors to take my suspicions seriously.

Without speaking, the man wheeled off to his room and returned with a small pamphlet. It was published by the American Medical Association, and in it were the words I'd been waiting to see. An excerpt from the publication reads as follows:

"If the disease (ALS) is suspected, it is not enough to differentiate it from other neuromuscular disorders. The examining physician must also rule out a number of conditions which, though quite unrelated, may produce symptoms mimicking those of ALS so closely that they have often been attributed to the latter. In other words, the presumptive ALS patient could, conceivably, not be an ALS patient at all. He or she may be suffering instead from the effects of any one of the following: an arthritic spur on a cervical vertabra; a tumor of the spinal cord in the cervical area; a vascular abnormality affecting the cord; parathyroid disease; heavy metal poisoning."

No longer could my doctors dismiss the presence of heavy metals as, at the very least, a possible factor. The following morning, when presented with the contents and source of the publication, Specialist #3 grudgingly ordered a spinal tap and muscle biopsy for the express purpose of metal testing.

Sporting a few more holes than I'd gone in with, I limped out of VGH glad to be going home, but even more glad to have finally been taken seriously. Unfortunately, it had taken a year and a half to be heard (more than half the average life-expectancy for ALS). So much for early detection!

Once home, I settled in to wait for my test results. Was I to remain on death row, or would I be granted a last-minute reprieve? The vigil ended a few weeks later when neither my spinal fluid nor tissue culture revealed anything out of the ordinary. Likewise, all other tests came back negative.

Since then, almost five years have slipped by, and during that time, two important developments have come to light. It turns out that while I was pleading to be heard, another ALSer (unknown to me then) was mounting his own similar crusade. In Victoria, in 1984, a retired naval officer named Ken Gibbs was also diagnosed with ALS. Soon after, Ken noted that a couple fellow sailors on his ship had also contracted the disease. In research circles, two or more patients from the same location constitutes a cluster, and to make Ken's five-year story short, a lengthy investigation revealed the largest ALS cluster in the western world. More than forty cases surfaced within the Royal Canadian Navy. The reason I mention this is simple. Due to an extensive maintenance project, all of these men were exposed to clouds of lead-laden dust. Coincidence, hey what?

The second and equally compelling development occurred much closer to home. Even though ALS is as common as Multiple Sclerosis, it's still considered rare. I'll let you be the judge of what's rare and what isn't, but because I seldom stray beyond my very rural surroundings, I've had virtually no contact with other ALSers. The one exception to this lived about twenty miles away. Graham Craig was also a young man with a young family, and before he died, his family and mine spent a few afternoons visiting back and forth. On one of those visits I asked Graham if the inhalation of diesel exhaust had played any significant role in his past. I remember him laughing off my question as the understatement of the year. Like me, his work life had begun in his father's logging camp, and while there, he'd spent countless hours running a log loader that just happened to be notorious for its faulty exhaust system. Graham told me of conditions so severe that on one occasion, in a hazy stupor, he slid right off the operator's seat. Luckily, striking the floor rallied him enough to shut off the machine and step out for some much-needed air.

When your number is up, your number is up, and at this

point I must stress that I've come to accept being the one in twelve thousand who gets ALS. I've even learned to accept being the one in twelve thousand who just happened to spend countless hours skippering a one-of-a-kind smoke bomb of a boat, but as long as I live, I will never accept being the one in twelve thousand whose closest one in twelve thousand acquaintance also just happened to spend a good part of his life choking on diesel exhaust.

In hindsight, it's important to understand that by making my suspicions known, I'd hoped to be welcomed as someone trying to help. Instead, I've come to believe that in cases of incurable disease, the hierarchical gulf between doctors and us common folk is, in terms of research, patently counterproductive. Even so, don't think for one minute that I'm claiming to have found the cause of ALS. I'll be happy if publicity over the Navy cluster finally prompts some researcher somewhere to rethink the whole question of metal poisoning. But I do know, in my heart of hearts, that if finding a cure depends on the free flow of information, doctors must foster a climate where all-important clues can be more easily heard. Simply listening is not enough! To truly learn from what patients have to say, doctors must lower themselves close enough to hear.

To summarize, when told that articles and medical references supporting my argument were a matter of public record, the common response was, "Don't believe everything you read." When repeatedly presented with the severity of my work environment, I got responses like, "ALS doesn't target people who direct traffic, why would you be any different?" Comparing my situation to that of someone standing in the street should have infuriated me, but in the end, comparisons like this only served to spotlight my own stupidity. All along, I'd proceeded on the assumption that my doctors understood what I was talking about. How could they? Not only was I foolish enough to subject myself to a deplorable situation in the first place, I was expecting people who wash their hands before they work to somehow mentally absorb years of industrial filth. Even though, between them, my specialists shared well over twenty-five years of higher learning, they were no more able to understand the grimy reality of my world than I was to understand the meticulous sterility of theirs.

Surely, if the compassion and dedication that supposedly drives our medical community could somehow be tempered with a mandatory course in plain old humility, the system as a whole would be the better for it. I can't help thinking that, as it stands now, if and when a cure is found, it will be in spite of the status quo, not because of it.

In the meantime, one consolation is knowing that behind all the certificates and sanctimony are the fragile egos of mere mortals. In fact, with the exception of a few minor perks like luxury automobiles, sprawling homes, world travel and grade "A" beef, we really aren't that different. After all, these poor men hadn't actually asked to be placed on pedestals. I was just gullible enough to put them there.

The American physician Dr. David Rabin best described the intimidation of his peers with this remark: "The deadly reputation acquired by ALS has made it a pariah in the medical world." Perhaps his candid comment comes from a place not all in his profession can fathom. Dr. Rabin had ALS.

Did you ever do something on a whim and have it alter your entire life?

5

Going Public

The most common course for ALS to follow is straight down, a physical free fall that claims its victim in two or three years. I've come to liken my descent to that of a paraglider: slow at times, more rapid at others, even catching brief and gentle updrafts now and then, but all the while spiralling ever closer to earth. As my condition worsened, I found myself spending more and more time indoors, and more often than not, the radio was on. I'd never been one for top-forty stations; I usually tuned in to current affairs and open-line programs. As days became weeks and weeks turned to months, I couldn't help noticing the absence of coverage when it came to one issue that I considered kind of important.

In 1989, I wrote a letter to well-known radio host and author Peter Gzowski. For the benefit of the semiconscious, Peter anchors a daily program for the Canadian Broadcasting Corporation called "Morningside." It's one of those shows that covers everything from political scandal and natural disasters to the interprovincial demographics of homemade chili recipes. My hope was that by writing someone like Peter, I might draw attention to the scandalous lack of public awareness that surrounds ALS. The letter came at a critical time. I had reached a point where disguising my weight loss and difficulty walking was no longer possible, but I hadn't yet gotten used to the stares I attracted in public. I was becoming an unwilling side show, and it was this self-conscious sense of freakishness that led me to sign my letter "The Incredible Shrinking Man." The name stuck.

I'd never really written anything before, so it was a bit of a shock when I heard my first effort suddenly airing from coast to coast. For a day or two, my head swelled up so bad that Ruth had problems squeezing me from one room to the next, but I never lost sight of the value of what had happened. Several times since, Peter and his staff have kindly made my letters and feelings nationally known.

The common thread in all the letters was awareness, but collectively, they serve as a sort of attitudinal altimeter on that paraglider I mentioned earlier. If I can stretch the metaphor still further, I look back on each letter as a precious updraft, and by scattering them through the rest of the book, I hope to provide a bird's-eye view of some key turning points along my glidepath…places to hover momentarily.

CBC "Morningside"

Hi Peter,

My name is Dennis Kaye. I'm just over five foot ten with brown hair and blue eyes. I like to think of myself as an okay guy, but unfortunately, at thirty-four years old, I'm dying. Anyone who can spell Gzowski has to be reasonably adaptable, but even I find this whole dying thing an imposition. The fact is, a terminal diagnosis can ruin your whole day. The vast majority of people with my condition last three years or less, so you could say that, in my fourth year, I'm on the home stretch. If you'll allow me, I'd like to use your voice and program to fire a couple of public pot-shots.

Does the name Muscular Dystrophy ring a bell? How about Multiple Sclerosis? Of course they do. These names and others, like Cerebral Palsy, Cystic Fibrosis, Alzheimer's, Parkinson's, (the list goes on) all have something in common. The mere mention of any of these names will not only ring a bell, but will usually conjure up a variety of clear images. I have ALS, and after four years of facing the ignorant and in some cases the indifferent, I believe both public awareness and the financial support that awareness brings are long overdue. When I mention ALS to the inquisitive, there are no bells. If I say instead that I have Lou Gehrig's disease, a few bells tinkle, but most often I still draw a blank.

To physicians, ALS means Amyotrophic Lateral Sclerosis, but to thousands of others it simply means slow death. Understandably, after reading recently that ALS is as common as MS, I began to think of myself as the victim of some cruel conspiracy. I decided to investigate further, and after careful study have come to this conclusion. Due to the high turnover of those afflicted, statistics only reflect the number of patients alive at any one time. Put more simply...they aren't counting the dead ones!

Children, bless their hearts, and related diseases like Cystic Fibrosis are quite naturally able to attract public support (and rightfully so). I don't act up, so I accept that a cure can't be demanded, but I find it hard to believe that the public wouldn't also respond to ALS if they were only made aware of the scope and effects of this disease.

Four years ago I enjoyed good health and performed well at a physically demanding job, but I need assistance now at even the simplest of tasks. This disease attacks the motor centre at the base of the brain and in turn, slowly robs you of all voluntary muscle control. The doctors say the end will come when the muscles controlling my lungs are affected. So with a keen mind, a healthy heart beating and eyes open, I will suffocate.

Now that you have the picture, I can devote the rest of this letter to the other people out there; the people who, like me, have grown tired of chasing magic cures, paying quacks and most likely have had a bellyful of denial. I'd like to pass on what I've found to be the single most effective treatment so far. It is, quite simply, a healthy sense of humour. I know it sounds corny, but like Reader's Digest says, laughter really is the best medicine.

A while back, while getting ready for bed, I was going through my usual contortionist throes of disrobing when the funniest thing happened. I was down to the second to last garment when suddenly, with one eye straining for the light at the end of the turtleneck and one arm almost free, my body stiffened. With one last desperate surge of strength I entered a horizontal, Pink Panther-like spin, coming to rest in a panting heap of arms, legs and underwear.

Any other time I would have slipped into an all-consuming melting pot of manic self-pity, but instead I was seized by the sweet slapstick of the situation. Laughter came grudgingly at first, but soon built to maniac proportion. My wife Ruth, who had by this time awakened, looked over the edge of our bed to witness my quivering frame and my face, still protruding from its polyester prison. Needless to say, she joined the chorus. Together we shrieked and howled until finally, out of self-preservation, our bodies automatically shut down on the brink of hyperventilation. When Ruth finally regained enough composure to pull the sweater off enough to see the look on my face, the whole foolery started anew…laugh, I thought I'd die.

It did eventually end, and when it did, I had discovered the true meaning of comic relief. The point is this: had I expended that much energy on any other activity, I would have been sapped of all strength, but instead I felt rejuvenated. It may not be a cure, but it's a damn sight better than anything the "specialists" have come up with.

This was no isolated incident either. I've indulged many times since that night, and the result is always the same: a genuine boost of energy. Like the time I became an eskimo in my own living room by accidentally flipping our wicker papa-san onto myself, but that's another story. To promote my treatment I even considered a career in stand-up comedy, but it's getting too hard to stand up. And as I'm sure the world is nowhere near ready for fall-down comedy, I'll have to be content as a household humorist.

My message is simple: lighten up. Humour is fail-safe, free and if you look closely you probably already possess it. It quite likely has just been beaten down by circumstance. It can not only make a seemingly unbearable situation bearable, but will, in the process, make life far more bearable for those around you. You still may not outlive your dog, but you'll have fun trying.

Sincerely yours,
The Incredible Shrinking Man

P.S. This letter was typed by pecking at my keyboard with a pen clenched between my teeth, so you might say you've received this information by word of mouth.

**Sometimes people do things that
defy explanation.
Other times we do things
that deserve one.**

6

A Grand Experiment

O ne of my early hospital sojourns was spent in Vancouver during the 1986 Expo celebrations. Every evening, just after sundown, an awesome display of fireworks would erupt over the city's inner harbour, and Vancouver General Hospital offered a free, albeit limited view of the spectacle. I would take in the shows from a coffee room on one of the upper floors, and one evening during the pyrotechnics, I was struck with a novel idea.

I'd heard the fair's planners had gone to great lengths to accommodate people in wheelchairs. Admittedly, my first instinct had been to avoid the whole subject of wheelchairs, but then it occurred to me—if life on wheels was truly in the cards, why not try a bit of preparatory education? Only through hands-on experience could I get an accurate feeling for what lay ahead. How would people treat me? What difficulties would I encounter? Would it be personally satisfying getting into really nifty pavilions ahead of everybody else?

I may not have been disabled, but everybody said I soon would be, and I figured that had to count for something. I also figured a monster medical establishment like VGH would probably have a spare chair kicking around. According to one of the orderlies, a storage room brimming with chairs was right next door in the adjoining ward. All I needed was to get on the good side of the dreaded head nurse. I had never met her, but rumour had it that she was tough as nails and twice as ugly. Back then, I still looked reasonably healthy, so convincing the horn-rimmed dragon lady that I needed a wheelchair meant looking a whole lot sicker. I considered pushing an IV pole into her office with a tube up my sleeve, but none of the nurses would give me one. Theft was an option, and getting all the patients to hold down their distress buttons could have worked as a diversionary tactic, but unfortunately, too many of my would-be accomplices were comatose. I even contemplated taking a reasonably conscious one hostage, demanding a getaway chair and seeking asylum in the Cuban exhibit, but discretion being the better part of valour, I eventually settled on the honest approach.

I found the door marked "Head Nurse" and knocked. A muffled voice said "Come in." As soon as I entered the cramped office I knew it was her—she had a tag on her uniform that said "Head Nurse." But this was definitely no horn-rimmed dragon lady. On the contrary, sitting before me, at a small, cluttered desk, was a surprisingly young and attractive woman. Actually, attractive doesn't really cover it, but despite her disarming smile, I remembered why I was there and wasted no time getting to the point.

"Can I borrow a wheelchair to go to Expo?" I blurted. To

my surprise, her instantaneous response was, "Sure, no problem." This was definitely my kinda head nurse. I'm sure if I'd asked for a triple bypass, she would have said, "Sure, no problem." At any rate, I had what I'd come for, and as quickly as she answered, I said "Thank you," turned on my heel and was gone.

Minutes later I was rifling through the storeroom in search of my prize. After a brief process of elimination, I settled on a real beauty. It had thick, padded armrests, a plush, form-fitting seat and sparkling chrome everywhere…the undisputed Rolls Royce of the wheelchair world. Instantly, the hall became my highway. I slipped into the driver's seat, fumbled awkwardly for a couple feet, shifted into invalid mode and was off down the hall like I'd been doing it all my life. I managed to make a perfect pest of myself for a half hour or so, until I felt confident enough to take on the outside world.

Just in case I powered out early, a friend who lived in Vancouver had suggested we get together, so we arranged over the phone to meet the following afternoon. Arrangements were also made with my doctors for a day off, and believe me, a day without tests was a welcome thought indeed. That night, as I scanned the skyline for the first signs of fireworks, I fancied the city lights to be the stars of an unexplored galaxy. Tomorrow, I, Dennis F. Kaye, would boldly go where no wheelchair had gone before.

Anticipation brought morning early. I remember starting the day as I usually did, staring into a pale pile of lifeless alien matter. It lived under a little stainless-steel cover, and at VGH, they had an interesting name for it. They called it "breakfast." I've always found hospital food to be a kind of culinary paradox. You usually go there to feel better, but somehow you invariably leave feeling like you've been on a starvation diet, hence the name "dietitian."

I'm convinced that somewhere deep in the bowels of every hospital are special machines. Feeding these machines at a feverish pace are small armies of sweaty, underfed drones. Trolleys filled with steaming plates of sumptuous food roll in one end and, seconds later, emerge completely devoid of any recognizable aroma or flavour. High-speed fans effectively eliminate telltale signs of warmth, while special detectors scan for lingering traces of nutritional value. If any stubborn vitamins or minerals persist, the offending fare is then repeatedly recycled by bulimic patients until it can successfully pass a stringent tasteless test. Once it's fit for the sick people, it's whisked onto carts for the trip upstairs.

This morning's ration was a wet lump of powdered eggs, topped off with a milkless bowl of cream of wheat (*mmmm-mm!*). Armed only with an impenetrable sense of humour and some refined white sugar, I did my dietary duty then headed out to call a cab.

When my ride pulled up a few minutes later, I got my first hint that luxury isn't necessarily what you look for in a wheelchair. The East Indian driver didn't say anything out loud, but as he strained to lift my portable throne, I heard him mutter something in his native tongue. Between his look of disapproval and the veins that bulged in his neck, I believe an accurate translation might have been, "No friggin' wonder the guy's disabled!"

As we pulled away, I breathed a sigh of relief. Free at last! While he dodged traffic, I made small talk, and in what seemed like no time, we slid up to a curb about a block from Expo's Main Street entrance. A couple huffs and grunts later, and my chariot sat ready and waiting. On the sidewalk, an endless stream of would-be Expo-goers migrated like lemmings toward the fair. I had reached the proverbial point of no return. In as convincing a move as possible, I gently transferred into what I hoped would be my rolling home-for-a-day. The driver hopped back in the cab, gave me a kind of "may Allah be with you" wave, and sped off.

I'd only wheeled a few feet before getting the second, even broader hint of my poor choice in chairs. Wheeling down the smooth shiny halls of a hospital was one thing, but this was the real deal. Suddenly I found myself in an uneven land of slopes, slants, humps and hollows, and the last thing I needed was a heavy chair. Calling it a Rolls Royce had been far too kind. All those chairs to choose from, and I'd managed to handpick the undisputed Sherman tank of the wheelchair world. By passing over the flimsy-looking stripped-down models, I had unknowingly sealed my own fate. In my haste to grab the big and the beautiful, I had unfortunately failed to consider one critical factor. I wasn't Arnold Schwarzenegger. Believe it. If Rick Hansen had used that chair, he'd still be slogging up a hill somewhere in Oregon.

So there I was...me against a thousand...surrounded on all sides. It was definitely time to switch to Plan B: boldly go wherever I possibly could. Despite my best efforts, every living thing, from parent-pulling pre-schoolers to old age pensioners, easily overtook me. I started to get a sinking feeling in the pit of my stomach. Even though the sidewalk sloped to the left, my chair had an annoying pull to the right. Unbelievably, the reason for the right-hand pull and the reason for my sinking feeling were one in the same. Now I ask you, how do you deal with a terminal disease and a flat tire on the same day? I had a pretty good idea what to do about ALS, but this new problem was a real brain-burner. To continue would be futile, but staying put meant certain death at the hands of the pedestrian horde. I manoeuvred as best I could to the edge of the sidewalk and bravely turned to face the onslaught.

As I paused briefly to ponder my predicament, to my utter amazement, standing like a welcome beacon barely three short blocks away was the towering sign of a well-known tire dealership. Suddenly the suicide option lost most of its appeal. I still had a problem, though. Wheeling there would have been not only physically foolhardy, but quite likely would have resulted in further tire damage. Clearly, I had no choice. With as much authority as any mortal man could muster, I stood up, assumed the pushing position, and with eyes fixed forward plunged into the oncoming tide.

From a distance, the whole scene must have looked like a page out of a child's puzzle book. What is wrong with this picture? One of these things is not like the others. Could it be one of the ten zillion tourist types walking the same way? Or is it the geeky guy with the empty wheelchair going the opposite direction? As I dodged and weaved my way toward my objective, I felt a multitude of accusing eyes upon me. I wanted to scream out, "I really am sick...honest!" but instead, all I could muster was an apologetic monologue of "Oh, excuse me, oops, pardon me, sorry Miss," and so on, until eventually I turned into the tire shop.

Wheelchairs work so much better when they have air in both tires. In less than half an hour I could be seen struggling along once again, but this time, at the same pace and in the same direction as everyone else. Things were looking up—in more ways than one. It was a real bum view from where I sat. Skinny bums, fat bums, flat bums, and every so often, a bum that made me glad to be alive. A few more minutes and I was there.

The Main Street entrance was a long row of turnstiles, each watched over by a blue-suited sentry. As I wheeled up close enough to see the whites of their eyes, a fleeting thought crossed my mind. What if they had ways of making me walk? Maybe they had disability police who poked you with pins to see if you'd jump to your feet? I had just started thinking it might not be too late to change my mind when a courteous young hostess called out, "Right this way sir." The lineups for the turnstiles were at least sixty deep, but all I faced was a professional smile and an open gate. So easy! I paid the fee, got my pass and wheeled through.

No sooner was I on the grounds than the smell of hot dogs filled my nostrils. Under normal circumstances, I would have been content to wait till lunchtime, but these were hardly normal circumstances. My desperate need for real food left me powerless against the scent's hypnotic effect. Its pungency pulled me through the sea of people like a flounder on a hook to a giant wiener on wheels—the mother of all meat-wagons. Once there, I wasted no time ordering. The day's first dogs weren't quite ready, so while I waited impatiently for my fast-food fix, I took in my surroundings for the first time. I didn't have to look long before the irony of what I was doing struck me like a pie in the face. This was a world-class exposition, for crying out loud. Virtually every noteworthy nation on earth was represented. I was smack dab in the middle of the world's largest international food fair waiting for an orange fuzzy and a bread-wrapped hunk of animal by-product.

Ding ding, too late. My processed treats were ready. When I wheeled over to collect them, I found out that all the fixings were around the corner on a separate counter. The counter was waist-high. Waist-high, that is, if you happened to be standing up, but for me, it was neck level. This instantly limited me to two alternatives. I could either eat a naked hot dog, or I could get out of my chair and go for the works. My preparatory education had just begun.

When it comes to the way we treat people in wheelchairs, I've come to the conclusion that there are four kinds of people in this world. I know it's shallow and unfair to start generalizing, but what happened next made me do just that. Just when I was about to write off the whole hot dog idea, a total stranger who'd obviously tuned in to my predicament stepped up to the counter. She grabbed all the condiments, pulled them out of their holders and plunked them down where I could reach them. Then she smiled and said, "Pretty dumb set-up, eh?" Before I could agree, or even thank her properly, she turned and disappeared into the crowd.

As it turned out, that woman was only the first of many people who would go out of their way to help me. People like these fall into what I call the Saintly group. In terms of empathy, members of this group seem to be light-years ahead of the other three groups. They don't read things into your situation. They see a need, evaluate it and immediately step in with unqualified support. Saints tend to look at people in chairs as just that, "people" in chairs.

Then we have the well-meaning Zombie group. This largest group consists of a broad range of people, but they all have one thing in common. They stare! Some of them would fix their eyes on me from a distance, and the closer I got, the more visibly uncomfortable they would become. Others would only stare until we made eye contact. Then they'd suddenly snap to attention, as if simply looking in my eyes might somehow give them a disease. Some would catch their children staring and reprimand them, only to stare themselves when they thought I wasn't looking. Still others would stare right through me. Even though I'd return their gaze, these Zombies would just keep on staring…studying me the way you or I might study a lower primate.

Considering that I still looked quite healthy, this group's reactions were the most surprising. I shudder to think what people with missing limbs or uncontrollable spasticity must endure. It's the Zombies, more than any other group, that have bolstered my admiration for disabled people, especially those with highly visible conditions.

Next comes the Oblivious group. This third bunch was pleasantly preoccupied with the excitement of the fair. To these people, I was nothing out of the ordinary. Compared to the Zombies, their nonchalance made me feel like a normal human being...just one more face in the crowd. Compared to the Saints, they weren't any help, but it's much easier to go unnoticed than to be the focus of unwanted attention.

Last, but not least, is the Ignorant Pig group. Your basic Ignorant Pig will stand at a crowded exhibit, notice you behind them straining to see, but refuse to give an inch. The Ignorant Pig will watch a heavy hydraulic door swing shut and walk away. Strangely enough, this group didn't make me feel out of place. I got the distinct impression they acted like Pigs around everybody. Besides, whenever a Pig did something really ignorant, a nearby Saint would shake their head in disgust and come to the rescue. Fortunately, for every Pig, there were twenty Saints.

In all fairness, before I finish my shallow, unfair generalizing, I should say that many of the Zombies seemed to be hiding something. I got the feeling that, deep down, a lot of Zombies want to be Saints but can't get beyond their own feelings of insecurity. They just don't know how to interact with real live disabled people. Depending on the nature and stage of disability, you may encounter the odd wheeler whose sense of independence is so focused that they'll refuse your kindness, but I can assure you these people are in the minority. Speaking as a reformed Zombie myself, I only wish I'd extended a helping hand more often when I was able—especially now that I know how few of them actually bite. Beyond this, all I can offer in the way of advice is this: Don't be afraid to take that first step. You just never know when you'll take your last.

Learning the ins and outs of life in a chair turned out to be a lot more tiring than I thought it would be. Around three o'clock in the afternoon I was thanking my lucky stars that I'd arranged to meet up with a friend. When I spotted her face in the crowd, I didn't have a hard time figuring out which group she belonged to. Her name is Jackie and her friendship was something I inherited when I met my wife. Ruth and Jackie go way back. I wouldn't describe her as the kind of person you ask for help. That's because she's always been in the habit of offering before you get a chance. Perhaps the best way to describe her would be to say that she's a hard person to be depressed around; her competitive wit and buoyant nature make sure of that. She also had a pretty mean cleavage, but in the interests of education, this too was something I would have to put behind me. If I'd been on the ball, I would have come in the kiddy-seat of a shopping cart.

I filled her in on what I'd seen to that point, which wasn't much. Lucky for me, Jackie worked for an inner-city courier service that just happened to make a lot of deliveries to the Expo site, so she really knew her way around. Now, I know I said Jackie was basically a kind person, but something about my wheelchair seemed to bring out the cut-throat courier in her. I've been with women in labour that didn't scare me as much as Jackie when her evil twin took hold of my handles and started to push. With my own personal saint/maniac tour guide, I was off at breakneck speed, weaving through an unsuspecting crowd. And speaking of crowds, in terms of sheer numbers, Expo 86 was the most successful world's fair to date. That day's attendance topped 200,000, which meant we had at least 400,000 innocent Achilles tendons to slow us down, 400,000 fresh, virgin shins and, barring deformities, four million toes just waiting to be run over. I lost count after the first few feet.

And that's basically the way the rest of the day went. Leaving a trail of battered victims from New Zealand to Nairobi, I cruised the world at an altitude of eighteen inches, courtesy of Air Jackie. We had Chinese food in China, beer in Bavaria, got off for a while in a Soviet space station, and somehow managed a four-point landing back in Canada when the sun went down.

We finished off the evening at Canada Place, listening to the then-unknown Colin James. As it turned out, the day was just a preview of things to come. When the Rolling Stones came to town a couple years later, Jackie got tickets and we did the same thing all over again...with one obvious and depressing difference in the wheelchair department. For the time being, though, it felt good to stand up at the end of it all, climb unassisted into a cab and head back to the hospital.

Aside from a few dirty looks at the public urinals, things had gone pretty smoothly, and all in all, I had learned exactly what I'd set out to learn. As for genuine disability, that would come soon enough.

That night, as I lay reaching for sleep under crisp, white sheets, I remember a mind cluttered with images: the sights and sounds of other lands, flat tires, spinal taps, pigs, saints and finally z z z z z z z

Things rock steady,
crumble and fall.
Things rock solid,
grow vague and vaporous.
That which once stood fast,
silently lifts, drifts
and is gone.

7

Change of Heart

September 12, 1989

CBC "Morningside"

Hi Peter,

Me again! I wrote you back in May with a crash course on the
effects of ALS or Lou Gehrig's disease. Speaking for ALSers everywhere, broadcast of that letter has not gone unappreciated. I
received letters and calls from across the country, confirming my sus-
picion that, not only is ALS an under-publicized disease when compared to other less serious afflictions, but that camaraderie among
those affected is virtually non-existent, simply because the comrades
are dying with such tragic regularity. One can hardly expect the victims, mostly elderly and dropping like flies, to have a united voice.

That a disease's very severity would be the single biggest reason for its lack of publicity is, to me, truly ironic.

Being one of the youngest people to contract ALS (29), I have a better chance than most to exceed the three-year life-expectancy. So at a cocky thirty-four, I feel a sense of duty to spout off for those who can't. If you'll grant me a second slot on your program I'd like to offer what, in the world of progressive disease, amounts to a "progress report."

Since my last letter the loss of strength has spread more noticeably to my speech, causing my palate to fall. This leaves me sounding kind of like Darth Vader with a harelip. Because I have to talk on one of those awful sounding speaker-phones, those who don't know me often think I'm drunk. Mind you, this can be convenient, because every once in a while I am.

My legs have shown the most dramatic weakening since May, and because my arms have long since lost their usefulness, it's making a difficult situation even more difficult. To better grasp what it's like, try to imagine yourself walking on a pair of stilts. In the middle of each stilt is a hinge. OK, what ever you do, don't lean back. Now, to complete the picture, on the bottom of each stilt is affixed a small but very responsive spring. Needless to say, I walk as if I can't decide if I'm on a leisurely stroll or dancing to La Bamba.

A few days ago, while heading for my bathroom, I ended up in a whole different room. I was just wobbling along, minding my own business, when suddenly, one of my stilts parted in the middle. I remember saying goodbye to myself in the mirror as I left on an unscheduled trip toward our bedroom. Thank God for walls. A couple well-timed rebounds and swan-like twirls later I landed spread-eagled and face down on top of our bedside table. As I lay there like a turtle with its shell on backwards, I heard this sarcastic voice inside me say, "And now, for my next trick." Within seconds my wife and daughters came to the rescue and helped me to my feet.

Much later, after I'm sure everyone else was asleep, I decided it was time for a wheelchair. The one I'm rumoured to be getting is an all-terrain model so I'm sure that new adventures lie ahead. I'll keep you posted.

Sincerely yours,

The Incredible Shrinking Man

As corny as it sounds, no matter how dark the clouds get, there truly is a silver lining...even with ALS. Before D-Day, my work took me away from my family far too much. It was commonplace to head out the door before my kids were awake and return long after they'd been put to bed. ALS changed all that. Now I'm home to watch my daughters grow. Change is showing itself on many fronts, and life is proving to be filled with trade-offs.

I may not be able to walk on the beach or play a game of softball, but let's face it, I can't shovel snow or take out the garbage, either. I've always wanted to be able to sleep in without feeling guilty. Now I can, and do, whenever I feel the urge. I used to fantasize about being hand-fed grapes and being showered by a naked woman. Now I get both on a regular basis. All I need to complete the picture is a manservant fanning me with a big palm leaf.

Please don't misunderstand me—ALS is definitely no picnic. But if I look on the bright side, my chances of getting rheumatism or Alzheimer's disease are almost nil. Speaking of Alzheimer's, someone dropped an interesting question in my lap recently. This person sometimes plays a troubling game in her mind where she tries to quantify the more desirable way of living out one's final years: mentally healthy in a disintegrating body, or physically healthy in a disintegrating mind. Even with the benefit of first-hand experience in the former, I found her question genuinely perplexing, and each time I play her game, I end up wandering into the same dark, dead-end corner. It's almost like I subconsciously checkmate myself to avoid thinking the unthinkable.

Perhaps I'm speaking out of turn, but as I understand progressive dementia, the more a victim loses, the less able they are to recognize their loss. On the surface, losing sight of one's own demise might seem like a blessing, but given the choice and what I know now, I probably wouldn't trade places for a minute. With ALS, the more I lose, the more I'm able to recognize my loss. If we're really just the sum of our thoughts, then I'd even go so far as to say that the more I shrink on one front, the more I grow on another. And because I'm no longer able to create memorable moments with any degree of spontaneity, memories have become infinitely more precious to me, so the thought of losing my past is too frightening to comprehend.

Change has come on a very immediate level, too. It would appear that many of us, especially men, see sensitivity and strength as opposing forces. Open displays of emotion are regarded as signs of weakness, but if you have ALS, you had better get used to it. Without muscle it's difficult, if not impossible, to effectively express anger and rage. Likewise, without muscle, holding grief, melancholy, even inappropriate laughter inside can be equally difficult. Although I've always considered emotions to be strictly cerebral, ALS has taught me that there's a purely physical side to emotion as well. In fact, you'd be surprised just how many muscles it takes to hold our emotions within socially acceptable boundaries. Without muscle, tears come too easily. The other night the kids and I were watching *Anne of Green Gables*. There's a particularly moving scene in one episode where Matthew Cuthbert is walking in a hay field. Suddenly he clutches his heart and falls to the ground. Anne runs to his side, and with tall grass gently swaying around them, Matthew dies in her arms. Then, as Anne softly weeps, the camera slowly pulls up higher and higher until, from a distance, they seem as small and vulnerable as two kindred spirits could be.

There's something about that scene that just does me in, but years earlier when the same series first aired, even though it did me just as "in," my outer response was completely different. My armour was intact then. I could tighten the muscles in my chest, purse my lips, freeze my expression, and in so doing, effectively conceal all sign of sentiment.

These days it's not so easy. Most of the muscle in my chest has disappeared, leaving my respiration shallow and calculated. Likewise, my facial muscles are failing and often cramp without warning (so much for a stiff upper lip). I'm also losing my gag reflex, so when I get choked up, it's more than just a figure of speech. And speaking of speech, perhaps nowhere is our physical and emotional behaviour more closely linked than during conversation. Although we usually attribute the execution of speech to vocal cords and tongue movement, it also requires a constant and intricate display of respiratory control. But like I said, my lungs ain't what they used to be, so the slightest stress or tension produces an instant and audible loss of enunciation, grammatical continuity and tonal clarity.

In 1986 I stood up to speak at my wedding. I was nervous as hell, but no one had any problem understanding me. A year or so later my voice started showing its first signs of weakness, so when one of our oldest and dearest friends asked if I could say a few words at her husband's boat-launching, I regretfully declined. I knew that as soon as I got nervous (it was a given) my voice would start to fail me.

A year or so later, during my first TV interview, I was no more nervous than at my wedding, but it took a concerted effort to make myself understood. A year or so later, during my second TV interview, I was no more nervous than at my wedding, but the producer thought it best to use subtitles. A year or so later, during my third TV interview, once again I was no more nervous than at my wedding, but all I could do was squeak. Very soon, if I get nervous, you won't be able to hear me at all.

The whole point being, in terms of emotion, I've become the proverbial open book. If something even marginally moving disturbs, inspires or touches me in any way, my forehead goes all crinkly, the corners of my mouth droop, my chin starts to quiver and my eyes well up like somebody stole my last cookie. It doesn't take much either. When Lieutenant Worf resigned Starfleet to defend his Klingon homeland I could barely contain my grief. Needless to say, every time Oprah reunites another one of her broken families, the floodgates open and I'm reduced to a blubbering basket-case.

And laughter is basically the same story. After all, what could be more physical than a gut-busting, side-splitting, knee-slapping fit of laughter? The problem is, laughing sends my guts into spasm, I can't hold my sides, and I haven't been able to slap anything for years. Instead, laughter for me comes out like some kind of moronic mating display. I shake and shiver like I'm trying to launch my own personal ICBM (inter-continental bowel movement). And my neck muscles have gotten so weak, I run the very real risk of laughing my head off. I honk. I wheeze. I drool. It's as if my feelings have taken fluid form—fluid devoid of all surface tension. One little jiggle and my mirth spills over in every direction.

Adapting to changes like these has gotten to be second nature. So much so that at times it's hard to remember how being healthy ever felt. Even simple things like opening a beer or closing a book are getting more and more difficult to reconstruct in my mind.

For those of us with ALS, or any progressive disease for that matter, self-examination also gets to be second nature. One finds oneself continuously looking inward for further signs of deterioration, and it's easy to lose sight of everything outside one's own sphere. And yet, even in the midst of all this navel-gazing, it's hard to ignore that the changes affect far more than just yourself. Everything you do, see, feel, even think is in one way or another inseparably linked to your primary caregiver.

Maternally, Ruth is a mother of two, but with me around, she's really more like a mother of three. Our daughters, Rebecca (thirteen) and Michalla (nine), are both vibrant, healthy young girls, but their Dad is a completely different story. I am, in every sense of the words, a big baby, a ninety-pound infant, and as is the case with any helpless child, Mommy must spend her every waking moment hovering close by. What if my nose should run? What if I should drool or, heaven forbid, what if I should have to go wee-wee?

The fact is, Ruth's time hasn't been her own for years. She gets me up, dresses me, bathes me, shaves me, combs my hair, brushes my teeth, cooks my meals, feeds me, pours my drinks, answers my calls, lifts my spirits, drops my drawers and, yes, helps me on and off the toilet. You name it, Ruth does it. At day's end, she wheels me back to our bedroom, undresses me and tucks me in. In her spare time, she does housework and all the other things it takes to hold a low-income household together. Almost every month my real mother spends a week or so lending a hand, and twice a week, a homemaker drops in so Ruth can grab a few hours of private time, but this so-called "private time" is invariably spent grocery shopping, paying bills and running errands. Technically, I suppose she does get away from me, but even on these so-called respite days, people somehow see to it that

I'm not really left behind. All too often it's, "Hi Ruth, how's Dennis?" or "Nice weather eh, how's Dennis?" or "I heard you guys moved, how does Dennis like it?" I'm sure sometimes she'd like to snap back, "I'm just out for a breath of air, and yes, Dennis is still breathing too!" I know people mean well, but they tend to forget that while I may be dying of ALS, Ruth is the one who has to live with it. Ruth is the one with the malignant growth in her living room—the thing that wouldn't die.

Change—adapt—change—adapt—change—adapt. My hands are so thin now that I wear my wedding band on a neck chain, but even that is a constant reminder of just how lucky I really am. Don't mistake my lavish praise for a declaration of Ruth's sainthood, though. There are days when I'm sure she'd just as soon slip something into my cream of wheat. I know of a woman who was diagnosed with ALS recently, and when her husband found out what lay ahead, he packed his bags, turned tail and ran. When it comes to matters of love, I learned early in life how words can often mean nothing at all. So in these times of cheap talk and failed marriages, I draw comfort from a soulmate who actually meant those time-worn words, "In sickness and in health."

Change—adapt—change—adapt. When I lost the ability to hold a comb, I started wearing a ponytail. When holding a razor got to be too much, I grew a beard. And because I can't pull up my fly any more, I have to wear jogging pants (like I'm going to go jogging). Come to think of it, what a great idea for a fundraiser—a Special Olympics for people with ALS! We could have events like the cryathalon, the hundred-yard stare, non-contact boxing. Or how about the hop, skip and jump—the hopping, skipping and jumping parts could be optional. But I digress…the point I'm trying to make is that I've never really been a beard/ponytail/jogging pants kinda guy. Now, between my hair, beard and ill-fitting clothing, when Ruth gets me up in the morning, the guy in the mirror looks like a cross between Charlie Manson and somebody off a famine relief poster. Reflections can be deceiving, though, and when I look beyond my pitiful exterior, somehow the Dennis who stares back still seems like the same old me. I guess some things never change.

CBC "Morningside"

Dear Peter,

Me again! I got my wheelchair. It's electric and goes like hell. Day before yesterday was my first day out in months. It was great! The kids tied their old tricycle to the back of the chair, so with one daughter clinging to my seat, the other riding chariot-style on the trike and me playing Mario Andretti, we were off on the infamous "Backyard Grand Prix."

It's hard to explain how wonderful it felt to be the source of my children's fun again. The checkered flag finally fell when we rounded a tricky corner at the end of the garden. Lying in the tall grass, and stretching from our house to the garden fence, was a water hose. Unfortunately, all good hoses have to come to an end, and when this one did, I had succeeded in momentarily tight-lining tricycle and daughter in mid-air. I turned just in time to see the strangest look come over her face as she tried, mid-flight, to calculate the unavoidable gravity of the situation. The grass was not only tall, but very wet, and as she lay sprawling and soaked, she looked up through crocodile tears and vowed never to forgive me. It was a good two hours before she finally did, and she was heard today asking when we could take the wheelchair out again.

Since my last letter, the disease's progression has been somewhat slow in terms of strength loss, but a visual appraisal of my body reveals a continued loss of weight. My pelvis and shoulder bones protrude now so that my skin is beginning to look like it's been draped on. My face is sinking and my lower arms especially have become very thin. In short, I'm starting to look a lot like someone waiting to be freed from Auschwitz.

So that you don't think I've lost my sense of humour altogether, I thought I'd close with a joke:

> QUESTION: How long does it take for an ALSer to put in a lightbulb?
>   ANSWER: I'll keep you posted.

Yours as always,
The Incredible Shrinking Man

Storm clouds have gathered.
A hint of wind tickles my calm.
Shoulder to shoulder
my circle of friends draws closer.
I am a house of cards.

8

Chain of Charity

May 12, 1990

CBC "Morningside"

Hi Peter,

Here we are, one year since my first letter and I'm still kicking.
I suppose I'll have to check out pretty soon or you'll think I've been
pulling your leg. All too quickly, another year has gone by and ALS
remains a little known and poorly publicized disease, despite the fact
that it killed more Canadians last year than a multitude of other
better known but less serious conditions.

The pace of change in medicine is so rapid these days that I can't
help but find it both amazing, and at the same time, troubling. We've
come so far. A person can pour alcohol down their throat day after

day, year after year, and when the result is cirrhosis of the liver, a mountain of medical knowledge will instantly kick into gear. Likewise, after voluntarily sucking in thousands of cigarettes, our cancerous lungs will be bombarded with a barrage of high-tech and incredibly expensive bells and whistles. And despite a huge awareness campaign, those who refuse to curtail their high-risk sexual practices or puncturing themselves with communal needles will, when infected, not only tap into a monstrous lobbying force, but become beneficiaries of the most concerted research effort in history.

So as safety nets spring up all around us, and breakthroughs become commonplace, ALS remains on the scientific sidelines. Well over one hundred years since ALS was first identified, and there still isn't even a known cause, let alone a treatment or cure. I've been racking my brain for some means of attracting attention to our plight and would like to bounce a couple ideas off you and your listeners.

The first means getting a friend to coat me in crude petroleum and leave me on a public beach. Last month, during one of your interviews, Stephanie Hewlett of the Vancouver Aquarium conceded that it costs ten thousand dollars per year to keep one oil-soaked Alaskan otter in squid, shrimp and other seafood delicacies; six otter equals sixty thousand dollars.

To put things in better perspective, Dr. Charles Krieger of the University of British Columbia's Department of Medicine informs me that they operate under a research grant of thirty thousand dollars. Considering there are two hundred British Columbians (at any one time) dying of ALS, this translates into one hundred and fifty bucks a head. I've got nothing against marine mammals, but if a half dozen sea-otter are entitled to mega-money and twenty-four-hour care from the private sector, surely the public sector should be able to justify something similar for my species.

Failing this, I felt maybe a cross-country walk might generate some interest. My arms aren't strong enough to propel a manual wheelchair, and I can't hop, but my wife timed me a few days back and in thirty-five seconds I managed to shuffle all the way across our living room. By my closest calculation, I could make it from St. John's to Vancouver in just under one hundred and nine years, give or take a decade. OK, that's a bit unrealistic, but maybe we could make it last for the length of the CBC building. People could sponsor me by the inch and, hey, we could call it the "Man in Slow-motion Tour."

If all else fails, there's always good old-fashioned civil disobedience. I figure if a couple hundred ALS spouses and relatives were to deposit their limp loved ones on the steps of Parliament, who knows, maybe a few thousand pounds of fasciculating flesh would get someone's attention.

Sooner or later things have to change, but for now I'd like to close by dedicating this latest letter to my wife Ruth who helps me eat, wash, stand up, sit down and everything in between. And to my two daughters who come running every time I mumble.

Sincerely yours,
The Incredible Shrinking Man

Once every year, the Amyotrophic Lateral Sclerosis Society of Canada holds a national fundraiser called Cornflower Day. The cornflower is, to ALS victims, what the poppy is to our war dead. Much the same as on Memorial Day, across the country, volunteers stand in shopping malls offering little synthetic flowers in return for the spare change of passersby. The concept isn't terribly original, and proportionately, in this high-tech age of telethons and world-saving rock concerts, it doesn't raise much profile or money, but without it the Society would have no contact to speak of with the general public.

At any rate, another Cornflower Day has just gone by, and this year my mother, Betty, and number-one sister, Glenna, saw to it that I was well represented. Armed only with their smiles and a couple trays of flowers, they hit the streets. Their territory was a small town called Sooke. I spent part of my youth there, and over the years it's become somewhat of a bedroom community to the provincial capital of Victoria. Like most bedroom communities, on weekends it becomes a beehive of activity, and this particular Saturday, mother and daughter chose the busiest part of the busiest plaza in town. Mom picked the front of a large supermarket and had a profitable, but basically uneventful day. On the other hand, when Glenna positioned herself at the entrance of a busy liquor store, she had no way of knowing that, before the day was through, she would make a startling medical discovery of her own, a discovery so profound, further study could well expose an affliction more widespread than ALS itself.

Between loonies, Glenna passed the time by comparing the behavioural patterns of people entering the liquor store to those entering other shops nearby. To her astonishment, an ominous trend emerged. Among the majority of shoppers, nothing seemed out of the ordinary, but in particular and in alarming numbers, the booze-bound pedestrians displayed a disturbing series of strange and unexplainable symptoms.

As people neared the plate-glass doors where Glenna was standing, a noticeably disproportionate number of them would cock their heads to one side, fix their eyes on the ground, raise one hand to their heads and nonchalantly pick their ears. For lack of a better title, I've come to refer to this odd condition as Cock Headed Ear Ache Pickosis, or CHEAPO syndrome. In severe cases, the infected party would leave the store exhibiting all the same symptoms, except with the opposite hand, opposite ear and their head cocked in the opposite direction. I've coined this more chronic form the More Infectious Spreading Ear Rot Sickness, or the dreaded MISERS Disease.

Demographically speaking, it's much too early to tell if either condition is limited to the Sooke area. Perhaps the unusually high ear-wax buildup is due to some local environmental factor. The worst possible scenario would be that it's alcohol-related, in which case, Sooke could be the veritable tip of an epidemic iceberg.

Regardless of where research takes us, to MISERS and CHEAPOS everywhere, I not only offer my heartfelt sympathy, but urge them to seek help. Admittedly, little is known now, but with the aid of skilled professionals, and the support of loved ones, ear rot can be beaten!

A full day later, Mom and Glenna counted two hundred and six dollars between them; not enough to build an ALS research centre, but a tidy sum for a couple of novice panhandlers. The only reason I mention this ear-picking episode at all is because it is what prompted me to ponder the entire question of benevolence and, ultimately, to write this chapter. To give or not to give? That is indeed the question, and it's a question with far more levels than first meet the eye. The more I pondered, the more I saw the benevolence of others as links in a chain. I began to see this chain of charity linking fatally ill people to the world around them, and it's true, charity really does begin at home.

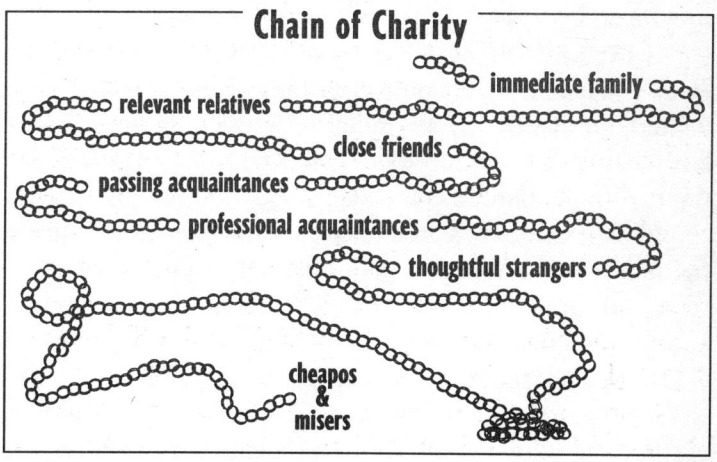

Chain of Charity

immediate family

relevant relatives

close friends

passing acquaintances

professional acquaintances

thoughtful strangers

cheapos
&
misers

For most of us, the first and most critical link is our Immediate Family. In so many ways, these are the people that form our first line of defence, but because most of us face death during old age, immediate family can be a rare and precious commodity. Parents are usually long gone. More often than not, siblings have their hands full keeping households of their own together. Children have a habit of moving away, and depending on your spouse's age, he or she may have already beaten you to it.

The thought of dying alone has a dismal ring to it, but both my parents are living, as are my sister, my children and my better half. You could say that for someone with ALS, I'm in the best of all possible situations. With all due respect to dedicated homemakers and nurses everywhere, if I had been forced to face ALS without my family, I don't believe I'd be alive today, let alone writing about it. Sometimes I wish I had one of those little push-button counters to keep track of how often I call for help. It's a pretty pointless wish though; I'd have to get them to do that too. Despite a million thank-yous, if I die tomorrow, it's quite likely my family will never fully appreciate how much they've done.

As I've said, almost every month, my mother (bless her forever-maternal heart) pitches in for a week to give Ruth a hand. Considering my stepfather is, himself, the recipient of a triple by-pass, and they too are on a fixed income, the four-hundred-mile round trip is no small sacrifice.

When it comes to Close Friends, sometimes close is just a figure of speech. Whether they're as near as a neighbour or a thousand miles away, just knowing you still occupy a place in someone's thoughts can help fuel feelings of self-worth.

Next comes the rest of the family, or what I like to call my Relevant Relatives. As if to separate routine from drudgery, every so often I get a call, a card, or a knock at the door, and it's these periodic contacts that have helped me maintain a sense of connection.

Passing Acquaintances, like ships in the night, seem to come out of nowhere, cast a brief light and, before you know it, they disappear. Like ships in the night, you don't feel their waves until they've passed you by, and they may not alter your course or quell the storm, but long after they're gone, just knowing they're out there somewhere has a calming affect.

Professional Acquaintances may be near the end of the chain, but they are important links nonetheless…especially the ones in the health-care community. If, heaven forbid, I should face my final days in an institution, several encounters with "the system" have given me an insight into what might lie ahead. It's unnerving to know that there will be those around me whose priorities land squarely between their last coffee break and their next collective agreement. But it's also comforting to know that there are those in the profession (many of them) whose palliative presence is a calling. Because they get paid, they don't necessarily fit the dictionary definition of "charitable," but in my experience, their spirit is as close to charity as it ever gets.

Thoughtful Strangers make up, by far, the hardest link to define. I've never met one. I likely never will. But each time one of my letters airs on radio or appears somewhere in print, I get a few letters and calls from out of the blue—rarely to sell me on anything—just thoughtful, warm, unsolicited messages of support. Like lifelines in the dark, I never see the face at the other end, but I know enough to hang on for the ride.

Where I end up on the last leg of my voyage may ultimately be out of my hands, so it's calming to think that before the chain breaks—before I slip into my vast forever—the last lights I see will almost certainly be those on a friendly shore.

In many ways, facing a terminal disease, has also forced me to face some fundamental changes in the way I look at charity. I was raised on good old-fashioned principles, and good old-fashioned principles dictate that charity is for the weak. Even though, physically speaking, I've become the proverbial picture of weakness, I'm gradually getting used to the idea that I might not be as weak as I thought. I'm coming to realize that true weakness is, for some, the inability to see themselves in anyone's shoes but their own.

Fortunately, not all of us are wired the same, and though it may sound cliché, even contradictory, for a lot of people, giving of one's self can actually be a source of inner strength. It's the theory of relativity at its very best: for every action there is an equal and opposite reaction; the more you give, the more you get; you reap what you sow; what goes around comes around, etc., etc. That old Beatles song said it best:

> ...in the end, the love you take
> is equal to the love you make.

I think I've always known this was true, but until this disease took hold of me, I never knew just how universal this principle really was. Ulterior motives notwithstanding, I believe the same principles that keep non-profit charities afloat motivate us as individuals as well. And just as an act of malice or aggression can scar us permanently, likewise, a simple act of charity can have an equally profound and lasting effect.

I suspect each of us has a kind of subconscious scoreboard where we separate the thoughtless from the thoughtful. It's where we chalk up all the little lessons along the way, and sometimes a seemingly insignificant event can determine the way we treat others for the rest of our lives. One such event happened to me in the mid-seventies when I was tramping around the British Isles. On the face of it, it may have absolutely nothing to do with ALS, but in my mind it goes to the very heart of "charity."

I had just hitchhiked from Dun Laoghaire on Ireland's east coast to a small town deep in the Irish interior. Athlone was only a few blocks square, but it had the distinction of having seven pubs, so it seemed as good a place as any to stop and sample some local culture. After settling into a cosy little bed-and-breakfast on the edge of town, I spent the evening meandering from one cultural exchange to another, and as luck would have it, I passed a little shop advertising "Bicycle for Rent." By this time I was so culturally enlightened I would have rented just about anything with a nice set of handlebars, but fortunately for the good pedestrians of Athlone, the shop had closed up for the night. On waking the following morning the bicycle still seemed like a pretty good idea so I found my way back to the shop, and by noon I had pedalled well into the countryside.

A few miles from town I came upon the slow, silent waters of the Shannon River and the tiny riverside hamlet of Shannon's Bridge. The hamlet's namesake was one of those little stone bridges you might expect a troll to live under...a picture-perfect spot to take a breather, so I plunked myself down on the grassy riverbank and pushed my shoes off.

Across the river was the village proper, a tight cluster of shops and houses clinging to the roadside like corn to a cob. Down the narrow main street a young boy lazily herded a handful of dairy cows. An old man plodded by on a rusty horse-drawn hay-rake and gradually disappeared down the laneway. For a guy whose days were normally filled with screaming power-saws and heavy equipment, this was peace. In my mind I often return to the banks of the Shannon, and had nothing else happened that day, its calming memory would be quite enough. But something did happen.

On my side of the river there was but a single dwelling. It was only a few yards back down the road, and when the squeak of an iron gate broke the solitude, I turned to see an elderly lady walking toward the bridge. In her hands was a serving tray and what appeared to be the makings of a meal. I took for granted that she was on her way across the river to visit a neighbour, but instead of passing by, she came straight to where I was sitting, and before I could even say hello, her heavy Irish brogue opened up like a flower.

"When I was young I used to cycle too, and ye build up an awful sweat, ye do. Once yer all filled up, just leave the tray on me gatepost, would ye?"

Then she placed her appetizing burden on the ground beside me, and as suddenly as she had appeared, she was gone. For lack of a better word, I was flabbergasted. On the tray was a piping-hot cup of tea, a big slab of strong cheddar, two thick, fresh slices of buttered, homemade bread, a knife, a spoon and a small crockery pot full of honey. I saw no legitimate reason why I couldn't be flabbergasted and hungry at the same time, so I picked up my chin and devoured every last crumb. After returning the tray I continued on my way, but to this day I still think of her offering as food for thought.

It's hard to believe it's been almost twenty years. I can still see the soft side of Ireland—the rolling mosaic of hedgerows and stone fences, the gentle pastoral landscape. And though the images have faded a bit, as long as I live I'll never forget the sight of that little Irish woman. Her kindness is with me still.

The first payoff in my public awareness campaign came in May of 1990 when CBC Radio devoted a feature segment exclusively to ALS. One of the "Morningside" producers asked me to write a "day in the life," and the following piece resulted.

LIFESTYLES OF THE SICK AND FEEBLE

Let me start by saying that ALS is not for the faint of heart.
In fact I only recommend it to those who truly enjoy a challenge.
After a broken sleep, interrupted off and on by severe muscle cramps,
I awaken to stare at my living-room ceiling. We no longer sleep in
our upstairs bedroom, as I'm unable to manoeuvre stairs safely.
Often, the first thing I feel is my face on a wet pillow. Most nights
I'm unable to contain my saliva, and this leads to the area around my
head becoming saturated in drool.

From both a physical and an emotional standpoint, I believe
these first few moments of the day to be the most dangerous. Not
only is muscular movement unpredictable, but it's the time I usually
question the importance of getting up at all. Walking is a balancing
act in every sense of the word and demands total concentration.
Because my arms hang limp, I am unable to protect myself in a fall.
The margin for error is minimal so the slightest distraction can lead
to a cracked rib or broken nose.

Once I've overcome the indignity of being washed and dressed,
I make the long trek to my office (it's in the next room). I wasn't
paid to say this, but feel it must be said: the first thing I do after
dropping into my therapeutically posture-perfect chair is clench a
pen between my teeth, take careful aim at my radio, and with one
rooster-like peck, turn on "Morningside." I operate a small video
production company. Before me is an array of dials and buttons, all
of which have been carefully arranged within pen-pecking distance.
It's here in my studio that I spend my days and evenings at computer
animation, designing commercial logos, editing and compiling video
scripts.

Around midday I usually break for lunch. On good days I can hold
a sandwich. On not so good days, I am spoon-fed and the weakness
in my neck and throat often leads me to choke. Luckily, spring comes
early on the west coast. My loss of body fat has left me very susceptible to cold, so after a long shut-in winter, on nice afternoons I'll take

a fresh-air break. We live in a very rural setting, and thanks to an electric wheelchair, I'm able to sit outdoors, think up scripts and watch things grow.

The last couple hours of my day are usually spent as a slouch potato watching the late news. The last major undertaking is getting across the living room to bed. While I lay there staring at the ceiling recently, it occurred to me that my condition is only an advance look at what most of us will experience sooner or later. I'm being granted a physical preview of what is usually reserved for the elderly, while being denied the wisdom that another fifty years would bring. Contrary to what my wife would tell you, ALS doesn't affect the brain, and I feel strongly that the single most effective tool I have with which to fight my disease is an active mind.

Each day I look in the mirror and see a bit less of myself, so it's very easy to slip into a state of self-pity. And while some may think I wear my sense of humour as a shield, I prefer to think that I brandish it as a weapon. If all goes well, I'll be writing you again. In the meantime, as long as my head keeps falling backward, you can bet I'll keep my chin up.

Sincerely yours,
The Incredible Shrinking Man

Saltspring Island, B.C.:
**Thirty-five years later and
I still can't pull up my pants.**

Saltspring Island:
**When I grow up I want
to sell life insurance.**

Isle of Skye, Scotland, 1976:
Footloose in North Scotland.

BEWARE
OF THE
BULL

Port Neville, B.C.:
Bucking logs at the beach.

Honey Pie.

Port Neville: **Working up a sweat.**

Honey Pie:
Look Ma no brakes.

Vernon, B.C., 1978: **Leading Ruth astray.**

Logging, 1976:
Is it any wonder Ruth fell in love with me?

Havannah Channel, B.C., 1977:
The barge I called home for 8 years.

Vernon, 1978:
Rebel without a cause.

Kelsey Bay, B.C., 1983:
Before the storm.

Havannah Channel, 1984: The *Joint Venture* bound for
Thompson Sound, Kingcome Inlet and points beyond.

Kelsey Bay, 1985:
Rebecca, 5 and
Michalla, 1.
Six months after
D-Day.
All cleaned up
to try my hand in
the beer business.

Kelsey Bay, 1986: **Another change of hats.**
Getting my video production business up and running.

Sooke, 1992:
Me & My Girls.

1992: **I get by with a lot of help from my friends.**

Rebel with a cause.

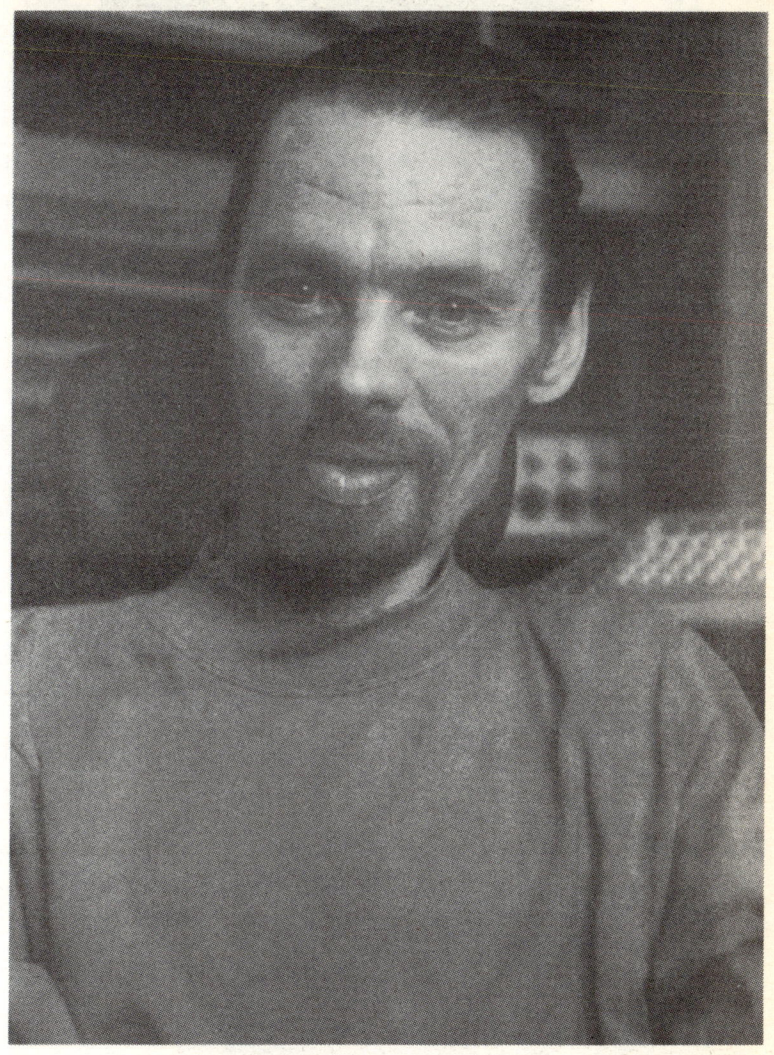

Victoria, B.C.,
August 1992:
Bid for Change.
Things start
paying off.

Quadra
Island,
1993:
**Ho hum,
another day
in Paradise.**

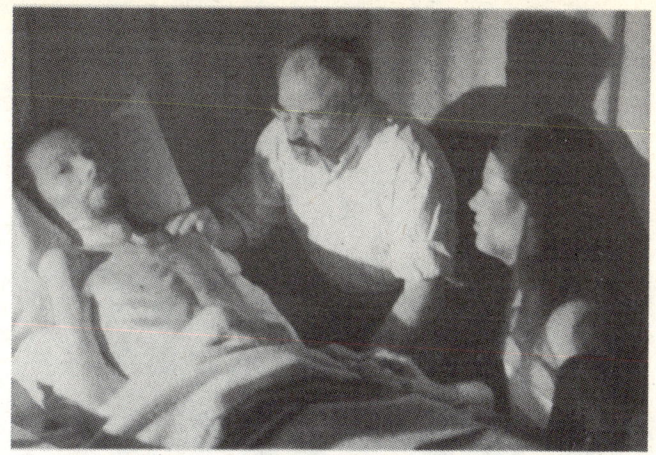

G.F. Strong Rehabilitation Centre, November 1992:
On the set of my latest public service announcement for ALS Awareness.

Vancouver, 1992: **Friends in high places.**
Independence '92—A presentation by the B.C. minister of Advanced
Education.

Quadra Island, 1993:
Our Island Home.

Part Two

The Practical Stuff

Another lingers in this room
Whose silent screams were never heard.
Television volume rising,
Game show hosts seem so absurd.

Spandex, latex, velcro world
Spotless windows, spotless tiles.
Television volume rising,
Vanna smiles and smiles and smiles.

Intravenous memories,
Frigid porcelain, stainless steel.
Television volume rising,
Barker makes another deal.

Hypodermics at the ready,
Ventilators suck and wheeze.
Television volume rising,
Heaven for a hundred please.

9

Getting Down To Basics

If you liked Part One, you should like Part Three. Part Two, on the other hand, comes with a warning. For the most part, its style and subject matter are factual, dry and purely educational. I realize the logical place for this kind of material would have been right at the end, but if you're like most people you might not have thought its clinical content worth wading through. Likewise, if I'd put it at the beginning, it probably would have turned folks off before they gave the book a chance. But before you pass judgment, you should know that I had much more than logistic reasons for arranging things as I have.

When I first started to formulate how this book would take shape, the pathetic irony of a stranger's anguish kept coming back to haunt me. Soon after writing one of my early "Morningside" letters, I received an unexpected response from a Prince George man who had just lost his wife, Aleza, to ALS. As always, the tone of the correspondence was one of encouragement and support, but underlying the man's message was an undeniable cry for help. Unable to care for Aleza in the end stages of her illness, he had grudgingly admitted defeat and checked her into hospital. To his anger and disbelief, and despite pleas to the contrary, he repeatedly found the staff treating her as though she were mentally retarded. Needless to say, his grief was compounded by an unwarranted sense of guilt over the institutional nightmare he had unwittingly inflicted on the woman he loved.

Up until the mid-1800s, ALS victims who weren't able to communicate were routinely housed with everything from the marginally unstable to the criminally insane. In fact, it was within the bowels of France's largest mental asylum that ALS was first identified. But the thought that a patient on the eve of the twenty-first century could still be subjected to such archaic ignorance not only touched a raw personal nerve, it exposed the desperate need for grass-roots enlightenment. People need to know about the nuts and bolts of this disease.

So it's the humiliation that that woman was forced to endure in her final days that ultimately prompted me to split my story with such an unorthodox interlude. By interrupting my personal account, I hope to provide a sort of literary stumbling-block—something the reader must visually trip over in order to complete the book. In so doing, I'm hoping a few people who wouldn't otherwise bother will make a conscious decision to educate themselves.

The advice offered has been gathered from a series of booklets jointly published by the Amyotrophic Lateral Sclerosis Society of Canada and the Amyotrophic Lateral Sclerosis Society of Ontario. Because ALS strikes in so many different ways, it's impossible to present an accurate picture for every victim, but by the same token, because the effects of ALS run a medical gamut, this section is a gold mine of helpful hints for many other similar diseases and disabilities. I myself am not following the most common course for an ALSer so I can't personally endorse every single word, but I can say with complete confidence that what you read in the next few chapters is an excellent rule of thumb. If you have a friend or family member who's been diagnosed with ALS, or have some professional interest, you'll probably want to flip back to Part Two from time to time. If, on the other hand, you have no personal connection and find yourself wanting to skip straight ahead to Part Three, think of Aleza, and the world of difference a little practical knowledge might one day make for someone you love.

What Is ALS?

Amyotrophic Lateral Sclerosis is a disease of the motor neurons in the spinal cord and lower brain which control the voluntary muscles throughout the body. When these motor neurons die as a result of ALS, the ability of the brain to control muscle movement is lost. The groups of muscles affected and the order in which they are affected varies from one person to another. For some people with ALS, symptoms begin with the muscles for swallowing and the tongue. For many others, muscles in the hands, wrists, shoulders and ankles tend to weaken first.

Because ALS attacks only motor neurons, it does not affect the mind. The person with ALS remains mentally sharp and in full possession of senses of sight, hearing, taste, smell and touch. Bladder and bowel muscles are generally not affected by ALS. ALS seldom causes pain, although some people do have secondary discomfort from lengthy sitting or lying down. Sexual function is not affected by the disease.

There are three classifications of ALS:

- sporadic (which is the most common form of ALS);
- familial (a small number of cases suggest genetic inheritance);
- and Guamanian (a high number of cases of ALS occur in Guam and the Trust Territories of the Pacific).

The cause of ALS is not yet known, although several theories are now being researched. At present, neither a cure for ALS nor a means of prevention is known.

Symptoms of ALS

The early symptoms of ALS can be rather vague. They include tripping, dropping things, slurred or "thick" speech and muscle cramping or twitching. Some elderly people with these early symptoms may assume that they are normal changes of aging. As the disease progresses, the muscles of the trunk of the body are affected. Weakness of the breathing muscles develops slowly over months or years and is experienced as a decrease in energy. Death from ALS is almost always due to severe weakness of the breathing muscles and a resulting subtle loss of consciousness.

Incidence of ALS

ALS is not a rare disease; it affects about six to eight people out of every 100,000. Most people who get ALS are between the ages of fifty to seventy-five, though there are cases of teenagers with the disease. ALS seems to attack men more often than women.

In approximately 5 percent of cases of ALS there is a hereditary pattern. About 95 percent are cases of "sporadic" ALS; anyone, anywhere can be affected.

The average life-expectancy for the newly diagnosed person with ALS is between two and three years. However, it is important to understand that improved medical care is resulting in longer and more productive lives for people with ALS. Twenty percent will live more than five years, and up to 10 percent will survive more than ten years.

Research Directions

ALS was first described in 1869 by Jean-Martin Charcot, a French neurologist. Since that time a number of theories about the cause of ALS have been advanced. Some scientists believe it is possible that ALS is caused by a slow-acting or "latent" virus, which suggests a chance that it is contagious. However, the theory that it is caused by an organism suggests that there is absolutely no fear that it is contagious, and in fact there is no increased incidence among medical personnel who deal with ALS patients. Work has also been done on the possible role of the thyroid gland and trauma.

Another line of research is investigating the possibility of environmental causes. The very high incidence of ALS on the island of Guam, in Western New Guinea and on the Kii peninsula of Japan may provide some clues about environmental influences. Heavy metals such as lead and mercury are suspected causes. So is aluminum, which can poison the body and cause ALS symptoms. Some people may have a genetic makeup which makes them susceptible to an environmental cause of ALS. Perhaps as research progresses, it will be discovered that the interaction of two or more factors may cause ALS.

Update: In March of 1993, the collaborative efforts of researchers in Montreal and Boston yielded the first meaningful breakthrough. A gene has been identified that, when defective, causes most cases of familial (inherited) amyotrophic lateral sclerosis. Although most cases are in the sporadic (non-inherited) form, there is no significant clinical difference between familial ALS and sporadic ALS. For that reason it is generally accepted that the familial ALS findings are important to the future study of sporadic ALS.

Your Emotional Reactions

ALS is a chronic and progressive disease. It is, as yet, incurable. When you are first diagnosed, your initial reaction may be one of shock. Although a person's reaction to a diagnosis of ALS will vary depending upon personality and life experience, there are some patterns that are common to many people. One of your early responses may be denial—"There must be some mistake!" Anger may also be part of your response. You may feel angry at medical personnel because they cannot provide a cure. You may also be angry at members of your family because they are not ill and cannot really understand what it is like to face ALS. You may later respond by feeling withdrawn and depressed as you face up to all the changes that will occur in your life. All these emotions are perfectly normal responses to a most distressing situation. For most people with ALS they are temporary, though from time to time you may have further periods of depression and resentment.

It is also important to be aware that members of your family and your friends are experiencing emotional reactions to your disease. They may feel guilty that you have ALS and they are healthy. They may also be short-tempered because of the extra daily responsibilities they face—banking, raising children with less help from you, more chores—all in addition to the care they give you. They may feel it is not fair, and then feel guilty about reacting this way.

Keeping the lines of communication open is the best way to work out these feelings. Talk openly to your family about how you feel and encourage them to share their feelings with you. If you find this hard to do, you may find it useful to talk with a social worker who is part of your medical team. He or she may be able to help you and your family solve your communication problems. It is most important that you have someone to listen to you who will not be upset by what you are saying or ask you to "think about something else." The person you need may be one of your health professionals, a friend or a family member.

Changes in Family Life

ALS affects not only the life of an individual; it also affects family life. For one thing, your financial role in the family may change. If you are one of the breadwinners, there will be the question of how the family will adjust when you have to cut down on work or stop work altogether. Perhaps a spouse who has not worked outside the home will become a breadwinner. Financial counselling from your bank or credit union can assist your family with money management.

Changes in roles bring emotional changes as well. You may have to give up a certain measure of financial and practical independence and rely on family members for help. For many people, adjustments like these can be very difficult. Your social worker can make you aware of what financial help is available from government and other agencies.

In spite of all these changes it is important that the person with ALS retain his or her role in decision-making. Your input is even more valuable now, at a time when so many important decisions must be made.

The Health-Care Team

Across Canada there are a number of ALS clinics that treat ALS with a team approach. In other communities, the same health-care professionals are available as individuals.

A variety of medical personnel can help people with ALS to cope with the limitations that the disease places upon them. A family doctor will refer patients to a neurologist, who is a specialist in diseases of the nervous system and can confirm a diagnosis of ALS. An important member of the team is the physiatrist, a specialist in physical medicine and rehabilitation. The physiatrist evaluates the condition of the person with ALS and decides which members of the team should be involved with him or her. In addition to the doctors and nurses, the person with ALS may deal with a social worker. If your person with ALS is experiencing emotional problems or if the family is experiencing stress, you may ask your family doctor or neurologist for a referral to a social worker, psychiatrist or psychologist. These people are qualified to conduct family counselling which may help family members to make this difficult adjustment.

An occupational therapist will advise about techniques and equipment that allow the person with ALS to continue everyday activities. The occupational therapist is also able to train the person with ALS and the helpers in the best ways to use various equipment for mobility, self-care or in maintaining the family's lifestyle. The occupational therapist may go into the home to see if the environment of the person with ALS will need to be adapted. It is very important to have the advice of an occupational therapist before buying any device.

A physiotherapist can teach range-of-motion exercises to maintain flexibility and to strengthen uninvolved muscles. The professional is also able to train the person with ALS and the helpers in the best way to use various devices that may be prescribed. A dietitian will assist in maintaining a balanced diet when certain foods can no longer be eaten because of chewing and swallowing problems. Speech pathologists help by training the person with ALS in methods that will enable the person with ALS to maintain verbal communication for as long as possible; they are also experts in the various communication aids available. The assistance of an occupational therapist is important in choosing a communication aid; the person with ALS must be physically capable of making full use of it. If problems with breathing are experienced, your person with ALS will be referred to a respirologist.

Some ALS teams include a recreation therapist to help the person with ALS develop and maintain leisure interests. A pastoral care counsellor may also be a team member. Your community health nurse is a good source of information about community services and he or she can be a good emotional support. Check with your local health services to learn what resources are available in your community.

10

Mobility Strategies

The Role of Exercise

The purpose of exercise for people with ALS is to maintain the strength of those muscles affected by the disease, to maintain the flexibility of muscles that have been affected and to maintain the flexibility of joints in the neck, trunk and limbs. It is important to realize that exercise will not strengthen muscles that have been weakened as a result of ALS. Once the supply of motor neurons that control a particular muscle has degenerated, it cannot be regenerated by exercise or anything else. However, the right exercise program can minimize joint and muscle stiffness.

Range-of-Motion (ROM) Exercises

A person with ALS needs to move each affected joint through a series of Range-of-Motion (ROM) exercises every day to prevent it from stiffening. Exercise will help to keep your body as flexible as possible and your joints mobile. ROM exercises are usually done systematically—the joints of one limb are exercised in a particular order before the next limb is exercised, and so on.

Specific ROM exercises are not outlined in this chapter. The reason is simple. Each person with ALS needs a program of exercise tailored to his or her individual needs and abilities. Your doctor and therapist will prescribe the exercises that are right for you. Your physiotherapist will demonstrate the exercises and ensure that you are performing them correctly.

Moderation in Exercise

It is important that all exercise be performed in moderation. Fatigue will only increase your weakness and rob you of energy you need for your daily routines and the activities you enjoy. If you find that your prescribed set of exercises tires you, talk to your therapist. Changes can be made that will eliminate the risk of fatigue.

Similarly, none of your exercises should cause you pain. If you do experience pain when exercising, stop that exercise and talk to your therapist. It may be that you are not doing the exercise correctly and some re-training is necessary. Or perhaps some modification to your exercise program must be made.

Recreational Exercise

If you enjoy such activities as walking, stationary bicycling and, especially, swimming, keep them up as long as you can do them safely. If you experience cramping or fatigue, do not continue the exercise until you have consulted your doctor or therapist.

Active, Active-Assisted and Passive Exercises

An active exercise is one you do yourself without any assistance; not every person with ALS can do a full set of active exercises. Muscles that are able to move a joint only partially need active-assisted exercise. A helper may assist the muscle through the movement, or you may be shown a way to do a self-assisted range of motion.

Passive exercises are done completely by a helper when muscles can no longer perform any of the movement. The helper moves the joints through their range of motion by manipulating the limbs of the person with ALS. Passive exercises work the joints but not the muscles. Your therapist will train your helper to do these exercises properly. The transition from active to passive exercise is seldom abrupt. You may find that you can do some exercises actively, some with assistance and still others only passively.

Some Exercising Tips:

- Exercises should be performed daily and should become a routine. You may wish to break up your exercise routine into parts to avoid fatigue. If you experience fatigue, consult your therapist for a change in your program.
- Do as many exercises as you can. Later it may be necessary to switch to active-assisted or passive exercises. Your therapist will help you make decisions about the correct limits of your exercise.
- Ask your therapist which exercises are the most important ones to do if you have a busy day ahead of you.
- Some exercises can be done while you either sit or lie down. Passive exercises are usually performed while the person with ALS lies down. Your therapist can advise you on which exercise positions are best for you.
- Stop doing any exercise that hurts and consult your therapist.

Posture Changes in ALS

If the muscles that maintain your posture weaken, you may have discomfort in your lower back, neck and shoulder-blade regions. Special cushions, chair backs, lumbar (lower back) and cervical (neck) rolls are available to help you maintain correct sitting posture. It may be necessary for you to sit in a reclined position or to use a neck collar to maintain proper positioning. Your therapist can assist you in choosing the right devices.

Conserving Your Energy

As ALS attacks your motor neurons, they become unable to send commands from your brain to the muscle cells they control. A smaller number of muscle cells must then try to perform jobs usually done by the full number. The result is that your muscles feel tired sooner than they normally would. One of the best ways to combat fatigue is by conserving your energy for really important tasks or for activities you really enjoy. Your occupational therapist can plan a daily routine with you that will help you adapt to life with ALS. Some tasks can be done in different ways, which will save some of your energy. There are a large number of aids available that can assist you to do things you now find difficult. Some of the more common types of aids are discussed below. However, it is essential that you consult your therapist before buying an aid—you may avoid some expensive mistakes!

Assistance Devices

Modified Tools

Many people with ALS have trouble with grasping and manipulating objects. It is often possible to modify everyday tools or to substitute specially designed versions of such tools to compensate for weakness in the muscles of the fingers, hands and wrists. For example, a knife, fork and spoon set with extra-thick handles can make eating much easier. There are also sets of cutlery available with long handles which compensate to some extent for impaired shoulder movement.

Mugs with oversized handles allow the person with ALS to slip all fingers under the handle, reducing the danger of spills. A plate-guard gives a slight vertical edge to a plate so food can be pushed against it onto a spoon or fork. The double action of gripping and turning a doorknob can be a problem for the person with ALS. A doorknob-adapter could be the answer, since it allows the door to be opened by pushing down or pulling up the lever. A fat wooden or plastic handle attached to your door key can help with the turning motion necessary to turn the key in the lock. Thick pens or pencils are easier to grasp than the usual thin variety, or a writing aid may be used, which consists of a block holding a pen or pencil.

Clothing fasteners are finicky and difficult to use if your hands and fingers are weak. There are devices to assist in fastening buttons. Velcro is a popular replacement for both buttons and zippers. Best of all, such items as pullover tops and pants or skirts with elastic waistbands need no fasteners at all.

Modifications to radio, light and television switches allow a person with ALS to turn the set on or off with the palm of the hand, a head movement or even a puff of breath. Telephones that do not require the use of hands are available. "Directed" equipment, for example, signals the operator with a puff of air.

These are just a few of the modified or special tools available to make everyday life easier for the person with ALS. There are many more such tools which your therapist can tell you about. Some are reasonably priced and some are expensive. Some will assist you for a long time, others may be useful only in the very short term. Your therapist can save you disappointment as well as costly errors.

A very useful book, *Help Yourself! Hints from the Handicapped* outlines many strategies for performing daily tasks in new ways or with modified tools. It is published by Health and Welfare Canada and is available from the government agency offices.

Orthotic Devices

Orthotic devices are aids that are attached to your body. They help support your joints in certain positions when your muscles no longer can. Such devices are usually prescribed by your doctor, and your therapist will fit and instruct you in proper use of the aid.

The "universal cuff" may be the most familiar orthotic aid. This straps over the hand and allows you to grasp such objects as cutlery, hairbrushes and other small personal objects.

A thumb splint helps in squeezing the fingers in opposition to the thumb and can partially compensate for a weakened grip. A larger splint can stabilize the wrist and place the thumb in opposition to the fingers, making it easier to grasp and hold an object for use. Many people with ALS experience "foot drop." This problem leads to stumbling on stairs or curbs. The answer may be a simple ankle-foot splint made of plastic, which is inconspicuous under trousers or slacks.

There are more orthotic aids available than we can discuss in this brief overview. An aid or combination of aids will be prescribed by your doctor. A physical or occupational therapist can train you to integrate these devices into your daily routine.

Canes and Walkers

A person with ALS who has weakness in one leg will probably use a cane to provide additional support. Several types of canes are on the market, both single-tip and multiple-tip. By shifting some of the body weight away from the weakened side, a cane can help to prevent falls. The choice of cane should be made in consultation with your doctor and physiotherapist, and you should not try to use it until you have been instructed by your therapist.

When a person is weak in both legs but still has good upper-body strength, a walker will probably be recommended. This spreads body weight over a wide area and gives the user great stability.

Wheelchairs

Many people with ALS will find themselves in need of a wheelchair at some time. Some will use it only for long excursions outside the house, some for certain activities only, and some people will spend most of their day in the wheelchair.

The decision about when to acquire a wheelchair is one that you will make with your doctor. If you always need another person to help you rise from a chair, or if you stumble and fall a lot, or if you are fatigued when you walk a distance, a wheelchair could be useful. No one is eager to use a wheelchair, and this is natural. But a wheelchair should be viewed as an opportunity to increase your independence and your ability to get around. It will also help you to conserve your energy.

Wheelchairs come with a large variety of features. It is important to understand that a wheelchair must be prescribed for you by your therapist. It must fit your body properly and offer a combination of features to fit your lifestyle. There are manually operated and power wheelchairs, chairs with removable arms and lapboards, and wheelchairs that can be folded up and carried in the trunks of most cars. It is very important that you purchase the right chair for you.

Many factors will have to be considered: your physical condition now and in the future, your financial situation and the availability of financial assistance, your level of help from family and friends, the sorts of services that your community provides for transportation of the handicapped. A wheelchair is a major purchase. If it is going to enhance your life now and in the future, it must be a careful choice.

Wheelchair-users will need ramps installed in place of steps around the home. It may be necessary to move furniture so the wheelchair can move about freely in the rooms. Publications describing home modifications are listed in the "Further Reading" section at the end of this chapter.

When moving from wheelchair to tub, toilet, bed, car and back again, the person with ALS will usually need a helper. Transfers like these must be made carefully to avoid falls. Your therapist will train you and your helper in the correct methods for transferring you. If you are moving to or from your wheelchair, it is absolutely crucial that the brakes be on and the foot-rests be moved out of the way.

Lifters

Lifters are devices to help with the process of transferring the person with ALS from wheelchair to bed, toilet or tub and back again. They can be useful if the person with ALS is heavy or if the helper is not very strong. The lifter raises the person with ALS in a sling so the helper can perform the transfer. Your therapist or nurse will show you how to use a lifter and assist you until you are confident with it.

Dealing With Problems

Falls

When a person with ALS has fallen, the most important thing to do is to help him or her sit in an upright position. The level of assistance needed will depend on the level of muscle weakness. Some people will need only some support while rising. Others will need to be lifted from behind until they can push against the ground with their legs. Still others will need two people to assist them back into a chair or wheelchair. It is important that helpers should not strain themselves but make the person with ALS comfortable until enough help is available. Ask your therapist to train you and your helper or family member in the best method of recovering from falls.

Muscle Cramping

Cramps are not uncommon in people with ALS. They can be alleviated to some extent by keeping the affected muscle warm and by stretching it or having your helper stretch it until the pain is eased. Severe or frequent cramps should be discussed with your doctor. There are a number of medications available to reduce cramping.

Joint and Muscle Pain

The "Range-of-Motion" exercises discussed earlier are designed to prevent the sort of joint pain that results from stiffness due to lack of use. Careful attention to your exercise regimen, whether active or passive, will eliminate much potential joint pain. However there are still a number of common pains that can develop. If your arms are weak and you allow them to hang unsupported from the shoulder, there is a tendency for the shoulder joint to become painful. It is helpful to support weak arms whenever possible on pillows, arm-rests or on a table. A shoulder sling will also give the arm some support and decrease strain on the shoulder joint while you are walking. Hip pain can result from prolonged sitting in a sagging seat or chair. A firm seat on a regular chair or a wheelchair will relieve strain on the hip joints.

If you are unable to move yourself you may spend too long in one position. This can be very uncomfortable both for the skin and the joints. Arrange for your helper to change your position every couple of hours throughout the day and to turn you at night. Some people with ALS improve their comfort in bed by using a sheepskin, egg-crate foam, a satin bottom sheet or a vibrating air mattress. Your nurse or therapist can discuss the options with you and help you decide what to try.

If you experience joint pain, discuss this with a physician or physiotherapist.

Further Reading

"Help Yourself! Hints from the Handicapped." Ottawa, Ont.: Health and Welfare Canada, 1984.

"Making Your Home Accessible: A Disabled Consumer's Guide." Ottawa, Ont.: Consumer and Corporate Affairs.

"A Modification Checklist: Accessibility for Disabled Persons Using the Residential Assistance Program for the Disabled." Ottawa, Ont.: Canada Mortgage and Housing Corporation, 1987.

"Specific Disabilities and Home Modifications for Independent Living: A Guide for the Delivery of RRAP for Disabled Persons." Ottawa, Ont.: Canada Mortgage and Housing Corporation, 1987.

11

Communication Strategies

How We Speak

Most people communicate by a combination of speech, facial expressions and gestures. Speech is produced by air which passes out of the lungs, into the trachea and through the vocal cords (see figure). As the air moves through the vocal cords, they vibrate and produce sound. The sound is then shaped by the muscles of the tongue, lips, teeth and palate into the different speech sounds.

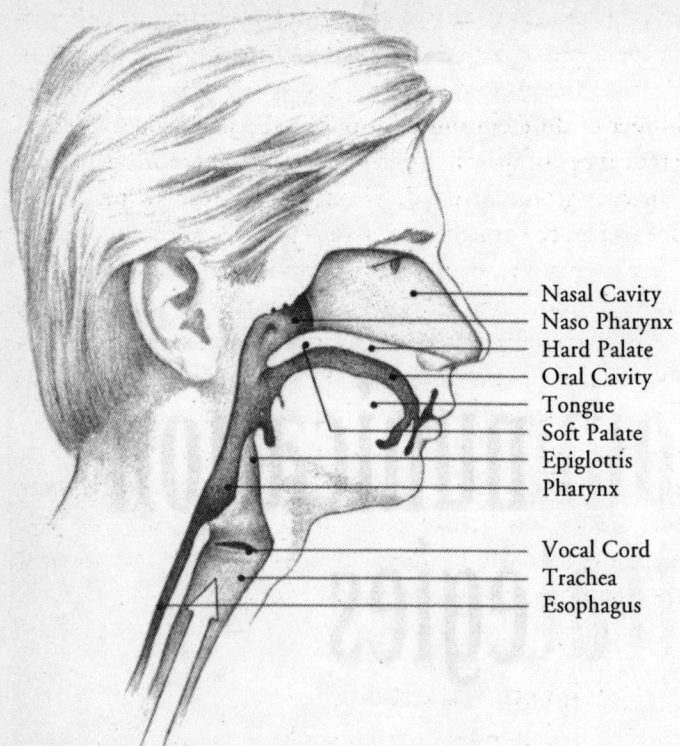

Nasal Cavity
Naso Pharynx
Hard Palate
Oral Cavity
Tongue
Soft Palate
Epiglottis
Pharynx

Vocal Cord
Trachea
Esophagus

View of the head and neck showing the parts of the body used to produce speech (epiglottis and esophagus are not used to produce speech).

ALS And Speech

Weakness in the muscle groups used in speaking can cause communication problems for the person with ALS. The term for this is "dysarthria." Dysarthria often accompanies problems with eating and swallowing.

Some of the muscles you use in swallowing are also used to form speech sounds. The next two chapters deal specifically with Eating, Drinking and Swallowing Strategies and

Breathing Strategies. If you experience problems in either of these areas, please consult a speech pathologist.

Because the production of speech is complex and involves a number of different muscle groups, ALS can produce several different types of speech problems, depending upon the particular muscle groups affected. Weak vocal cords can produce a hoarse or breathy voice. If your soft palate is affected, air may pass out your nose as you speak; the result is a nasal voice.

The lips and tongue form speech sounds. If they are weak, you may find it difficult to articulate well and to produce certain sounds. Your speech may be slurred and indistinct.

There are strategies for coping with these speech problems. Your speech pathologist may be of enormous help in training you in techniques to compensate for weakness in the muscles you use in speaking. He or she can also inform you about various communication devices available, if compensatory techniques are not helpful in your case.

Impact of Speech Impairment

The ability to communicate through language is a fundamental characteristic of human behaviour. Although many people with ALS do not experience speech problems, some are extremely distressed to learn that the degree of speech impairment has become so great that speech is no longer possible and communication must depend on communication devices. While no one looks forward to the prospect of using a communication aid, it is good to know that they are available, and that communication with caregivers, family and friends can continue even when the person with ALS can no longer speak.

It is an important responsibility of all caregivers and family members to learn any method of communication that the person with ALS chooses to use. Willing participation by friends and family can help to reduce or eliminate any feeling of isolation resulting from speech impairment.

Stephen Hawking is Lucasian Professor of Mathematics at Cambridge University in England and is widely regarded as the most brilliant theoretical physicist since Einstein. He has suffered from ALS for over twenty years. For many years his speech was severely impaired, to the point that he was incomprehensible to a new acquaintance. Since 1985 he has been unable to speak at all. But Professor Hawking continues to communicate some of the most profound scientific ideas of the twentieth century using a computerized communications program and a voice-synthesizer. He is strongly motivated to communicate his work, and his students and scientific colleagues want very much to hear what he has to say. The example of Professor Hawking demonstrates that, while speech impairment is certainly a challenge to communication, it is by no means the end of communication.

Some Simple Strategies

There are a number of straightforward steps you can take to improve your communication.

- Be concise. Get your message across in as few words as possible. Spare your voice by not rambling.
- Use non-verbal communication. It is not necessary to verbalize on all occasions. A nod, a shrug or a hand gesture can speak volumes.
- When you are speaking, give it your full attention. Turn the radio or television down or off. Face your listener; relatives and close friends often learn to be good lip-readers if they can see your face. Be very careful when speaking during a meal. If you eat while talking you may get food into your windpipe (aspiration) and choke. At these times, put the emphasis on being a good listener.

- Speak slowly, in short phrases, and pronounce your words as clearly and carefully as possible. Do not be afraid to repeat words that have not been understood. This strategy gives you more time to pronounce words precisely and more time for your listener to process what you have said. Careful pronunciation can compensate to some extent for weakness in your lips and tongue.

- If you cannot speak or write, you will need a code for "yes" and "no." Head movements, finger-tapping and eye expressions have all been used successfully. Be sure the signal for "yes" is distinct from "no." Friends and family can then phrase their conversations to include questions with "yes" or "no" answers.

- If excess mucus and saliva are a problem, you can use a suction device to clear your mouth and upper throat. This will make your voice less "gurgly."

- You can point to letters on an alphabet board that correspond to the initial letters of the words you speak. This will give your listener more information and may improve communication.

- Eating and speaking use some of the same muscles. If your muscles tire easily, it is a good idea to avoid speaking too much just before, during and just after a meal.

Using the Telephone

Telephoning is one of the most common means of communicating with the outside world. ALS can make telephone use difficult, but there are ways of dealing with many telephone problems.

- Your telephone system may be able to supply a button-operated phone which does not need to be held.

- Most telephone systems provide a relay service. Anyone who has a telecommunication device for the deaf (in some systems these devices are referred to as TDDs) may use this service. Here is how it works. The person with this device calls the relay service, types a message to the operator, who then relays the message orally to the receiver of the call. The operator can also relay messages back to the caller. Because the operator acts as intermediary, only the person with ALS needs any special equipment. This equipment can be purchased from the Canadian Hearing Society, and information about the relay service can be obtained by calling your local telephone company directly. A speech pathologist can tell you if this device would be helpful to you.

- A service called Directel assists the person without hand function who is still able to speak. It uses a puff of breath to signal the operator, who then takes verbal instructions to complete the call.
- A voice-amplifier can be attached to the telephone to boost the volume of weak voices.
- Emergency telephone communication is possible through systems that allow for automatic dialling of several emergency numbers and the playing of pre-recorded tapes.
- You may be able to use pre-recorded messages in your daily telephoning. For example, as soon as someone picks up the telephone, he or she would hear your message explaining your speech difficulties and setting up a "code" to be used for the rest of the call. A one-sided conversation could then continue, with you answering "yes" or "no" questions by taps on the mouthpiece. You can also use this technique to pre-plan "yes" or "no" conversation with close friends you call often.
- You can use a telephone answering machine to "screen" incoming calls and then decide which ones are important to you.

A number of telephone companies provide telecommunication services for special needs. They give information about special equipment that will make telephoning easier for people with hearing, speech, visual or physical disabilities. Disabled customers are entitled to discounts on certain equipment. To enquire about these services call your local telephone company.

Communication Aids

Communication aids range from the very simple to the extremely sophisticated. For the person who has good use of hands and arms, writing can take the place of speech. If you use paper, make sure it is well supported by using a small clipboard. A small slate board or a "magic" slate is portable and inexpensive. If loss of manual dexterity makes writing difficult, a typewriter may be the answer. Keys can be operated by hand or by a head-pointer if the user's hand and arm function is not up to typing. An occupational therapist can determine the type of keyboard required. While the ordinary typewriter is not very portable, there are portable tapewriters available, such as the Canon Communicator. These are about the size of a hand-held calculator and print out messages on small paper tapes.

Communication or alphabet boards can be made at home and are the most common aid. "Speaker" and "listener" see both the board and each other. Either may point to the letters that will spell out the message. A pencil and paper to record the letters is helpful. Communication boards have the advantage that both persons are actively involved in true two-way communication. And they are less expensive than some of the more sophisticated aids.

Microprocessor-based aids can be used by almost anyone who has some body movement. These aids use a computer memory to store words, phrases or even entire messages. The sender can create a message from an alphabet display. The message may be "spoken" by a voice-synthesizer or displayed on a light-board or paper tape. These devices can be very effective, but both sender and receiver must be committed to learning them.

There is a great variety of communication aids available, ranging widely in cost and sophistication. When choosing an aid it is important that you have the assistance of your occupational therapist and speech pathologist. The occupational therapist usually determines the physical ability of the person with ALS to use various devices. The occupational therapist and speech pathologist collaborate on recommending the more complex devices and training the person with ALS in their use. These two professionals will be able to help you choose a device best suited to your individual problems and abilities, one that will be useful now and for some time into the future.

12

Eating, Drinking and Swallowing Strategies

Bulbar ALS

When the muscles of the throat, face, neck and tongue are weakened, the person is said to have "bulbar ALS." Chewing, swallowing and control of mucus and saliva can then be problems.

Eating and Drinking

The Process of Eating

Eating is a complex process that involves several groups of muscles. Muscles in the hand and arm hold utensils and carry them to the mouth. Facial muscles shape the mouth to take in food and to hold the mouth closed. Jaw muscles control chewing. The tongue shapes food and saliva into a ball or "bolus," and then pushes the bolus to the back of the mouth. The soft palate closes the passage to the nose. Throat muscles produce the swallow that pushes food down the throat. Throat muscles also close off air passages so food will not "go down the wrong way." Finally, the esophageal muscles move the food down into the stomach.

Weakness or poor co-ordination in any of these muscles can cause eating and swallowing problems. There are many ways of dealing with such difficulties.

Coughing and Choking

In normal swallowing, the soft palate closes the passage between mouth and nose; muscles in the throat close off air passages to the lungs so that food will not enter them. If throat muscles are weak, food may feel "stuck" in the throat, or it may go the wrong way into the air passages that are not fully protected.

Coughing and choking are your body's way of getting rid of food or drink that is in danger of being aspirated. If you choke after swallowing, you or your helper should try to remove any food visible in your mouth with a finger. If food cannot be seen in the mouth, reach into the throat. It is important that your helper not slap you on the back—this tends to make you inhale, which will make the problem worse.

The best way to deal with choking is to try to relax and take slow, regular breaths through your nose. Lean forward and support your elbows on a table. This will allow you to take a big breath and strengthen your cough. "Splinting the abdomen" when you cough out will help to expel the stuck food. To splint your own abdomen, cross your arms over your lower abdomen and press firmly in and down as you cough out. Your helper can do this by standing behind you and pressing his or her hands flat on your abdomen. Ask your nurse or physiotherapist to train you and your helper in this important technique.

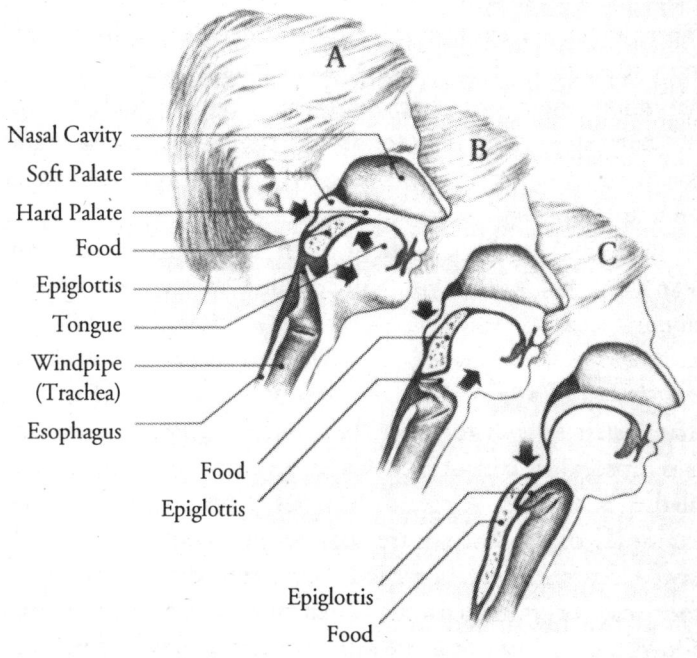

Nasal Cavity
Soft Palate
Hard Palate
Food
Epiglottis
Tongue
Windpipe (Trachea)
Esophagus
Food
Epiglottis
Epiglottis
Food

A: *Food positioned at the back of the throat.*
B: *The throat muscles produce the swallow and at the same time close off air passages.*
C: *Muscles in the esophagus move the food down to the stomach.*

If you often have trouble with choking after swallowing, consult your speech pathologist or occupational therapist. Also tell the doctor if you have noisy breathing or if you have a gurgly voice after eating or drinking. These symptoms may indicate that food or liquid has gone into your lungs. Often there are no signs when food goes into the lungs. Anyone with swallowing or speech problems should be seen regularly by a speech pathologist.

Dietary Changes

Nutrition is a very important part of health care for people with ALS, as it is for everyone. You should talk to your dietitian about the appropriate diet for you. Some people change the consistency of their foods too soon, when they could continue to enjoy a normal diet by making minor changes such as chopping meats, etc. The suggestions in this chapter are just the tip of the iceberg; your dietitian can help you plan your diet so that you will continue to meet your nutritional needs.

Foods to Include

The easiest type of food for those with swallowing problems is semi-solid in consistency. Casseroles, ground meat, scrambled eggs, yogurt, ice cream, bananas, pears, fish and jelly are examples of foods that are soft enough to be easily swallowed. Another possibility is the "pureed" diet. Most family food can be pureed in a food-processor or blender; this allows the patient to eat the same food as the rest of the family, but in an easy-to-swallow form. It is important not to process food too finely or to add so much liquid that it becomes watery. The ideal consistency is that of thick porridge. Foods that are too runny, such as fruit juices and broth soups, can be thickened by means of flour and cornstarch during cooking. It is very important to avoid lumps when thickening. There are also instant thickening agents available, which your dietitian can tell you about.

Foods That May Cause Problems

Not all of these suggestions apply to every person. Each person with ALS is an individual, and you should judge for yourself which foods you can handle. Common sense is the key. Generally speaking, however, problem foods include:

- Foods of mixed textures, such as soups with large chunks of vegetable or meat.
- Foods which become stringy, such as bacon, tomato skin or celery.
- Foods which form a mat in the mouth, like fresh white bread or well-cooked cabbage.
- Very hard foods, such as nuts, raisins, hard toast.
- Very spicy food causes some people to have saliva problems—others find it quite suitable.
- Foods that "crumb" when eaten, such as cookies, muffins or dry toast.

Liquids

It is normal to drink 1.5 to 2 litres of liquid each day. If you reduce your fluids, you may cause thick mucus secretions and constipation. If it is safe for you to drink liquids, have a drink at hand throughout the day and sip often.

If you use alcohol, drink moderately so that the side-effects will not cause you to swallow unsafely. And be sure to talk to your doctor about the effect that alcohol will have when taken in combination with medications.

Nutrition and Weight Control

You may fear that you are not getting enough food because you notice weight loss. ALS patients often lose some weight because of muscle wasting; your body can tolerate this. (It should be noted, however, that the small percentage of patients who survive longest will, over time, experience more dramatic weight loss.) Monitor your weight once a month and give the results to your dietitian or doctor. They can help you to adjust your diet so that you maintain your best weight. Nutritional supplements and snacking in general can help keep up caloric intake if you are losing weight. Supplements can be prescribed if your doctor or dietitian thinks you need them.

Some people gain weight, probably due to lack of exercise. Again, the key to this problem is good nutrition. Your dietitian can help you make any necessary changes in your diet. Excellent nutrition should be your goal.

Some Eating Strategies

Mealtimes are often social occasions, and, if at all possible, the person with ALS should be part of the family group. However, eating can be a slow and frustrating process, and it is important that you not feel rushed trying to "keep up." You may not eat enough or may experience coughing. It is important that meals be relaxed, unhurried occasions. If you find eating very difficult, it may be prudent to take most of your food with just your helper present. You can still be present at the family meal as a social participant.

In bulbar ALS, the tongue may be the first muscle to be weakened. The result is that food stays on the tongue rather than being propelled to the back of the mouth.

Eating is easier if you sit upright in a firm, high-backed chair, with feet flat on the floor and arms resting on a table. Your head should be upright and your chin tucked in toward your chest. This places the esophagus in the best position to receive food. If a supporting collar is used, it should be removed. A velcro headband attached to the back of the chair may be a helpful alternative. Ask your occupational therapist to help you overcome the eating problems that result from weak neck muscles.

Take small bites of food or sips of drinks; this will stop food from slipping into your throat before you are ready for it. Take your time and concentrate on swallowing. Try not to eat and talk at the same time.

If a full meal tires you, try smaller and more frequent meals throughout the day. Avoid activity just before a meal; come to the table rested and relaxed.

If you have difficulty holding utensils or a cup, you can try lighter cutlery with large handles and use a straw with your drink. An occupational therapist can make recommendations about appropriate tools.

Food should be kept attractive and remain a pleasure. If you are eating a pureed diet, be sure that the foods are processed individually and grouped on your plate in such a way that they are still identifiable. And if someone is helping you eat, ask that he or she present food from in front of you, not from the side, so you can enjoy both aroma and taste.

To aid digestion, sit upright for half an hour after eating.

Oral Hygiene

When your tongue muscles are weak it is harder to clean and lubricate your mouth. Dental problems can be the result. It is very important for you or your helper to check your mouth after eating and remove any food stuck between cheeks and teeth. Rinsing the mouth with water after meals is also helpful. The teeth should be carefully cleaned at least twice a day; electric toothbrushes, sponge-tipped "toothettes" and dental floss will be helpful. And of course regular visits to the dentist should be continued.

Constipation

Persons with ALS have a tendency to reduce their fluid intake because of swallowing problems or because they need help in getting to the bathroom. They may drop high-fibre foods such as whole-grain bread, raw fruit and vegetables because of swallowing and chewing difficulties. The result can be constipation. If you experience constipation, you can add fibre to your diet by using well-moistened bran in many of your foods. It can be added to such foods as cooked cereals, meat loaf and many sauces. You can use prune juice or stewed prunes as a natural laxative. If a liquid intake of 1.5 to 2 litres per day is a problem, use thickened fluids or foods that contain a lot of liquid, such as pudding or sherbet.

Your doctor may prescribe bulk-forming agents or stool-softeners if the problem persists.

Tube-Feeding

Persons for whom swallowing becomes very distressing or dangerous have the option of using tube-feeding instead of or along with eating by mouth.

Tube-feeding is a simple method of providing adequate nutrition (with multi-vitamins included) in a liquid form via a small, soft tube. There are many persons with ALS who live at home with their tubes and who maintain their lifestyles, including travelling, shopping and family activities. You should discuss such options with your doctor. Tubes of various sorts have been useful to many people but their use is often delayed because of unnecessary fear.

There are two common types of tube-feeding:

- a nasogastric tube, which passes through the nose to the stomach;
- a tube passing directly into the stomach or duodenum by means of a gastrostomy or duodenostomy.

It may be very helpful to talk with another person with ALS who uses tube-feeding and hear about his or her experience.

Excess Saliva or Mucus

Everyone constantly produces saliva and unconsciously swallows it many times in an hour. When the muscles that control swallowing are weak, you may not be swallowing saliva and mucus often enough, and they may "pool" in your mouth. Saliva may then dribble out of your mouth or down your air passages, where it can cause choking. Saliva and mucus buildup can be embarrassing and a nuisance. Most people use paper towels to absorb excess saliva. It is important to note that the problem is often transitory and may lessen over a period of months.

Some Suggestions:

- You may be able to control excess saliva by becoming aware of the problem and making a very conscious effort to swallow it every minute or so. If you can keep your lips firmly closed, this will also help.

- If this method does not solve the problem, there are drugs available that dry the mouth by reducing the amount of saliva you produce. Your doctor will be able to give you details about these medications.

- Suctioning will remove excess saliva from the mouth or uncomfortable amounts of mucus from the back of the mouth. Suction equipment acts very much like a dentist's suction tube; it consists of a motor, collection bottle, tubing and catheters. Talk to your physiotherapist or nurse about suction equipment; he or she will be able to tell you or your helper where to get the equipment and how to use it properly.

Dry Mouth

If you have a dry mouth you can get relief by sipping on ice water (if you can easily swallow it) or by using sponge-tipped "toothettes" dipped in water or your preferred mouthwash. Some people with ALS get relief with a spray bottle of mouth lubricant. Ask your doctor if some of your medications could be contributing to dry mouth. And ensure that your home and especially your bedroom have an adequate level of humidity.

Further Reading

"Meals for Easy Swallowing," V. Appel, et al. Houston, Texas: ALS Clinic, Department of Neurology,
The Neurosensory Center, 1987.

"Blenderized Diet: Easy and Nutritious." Toronto, Ontario: Canadian Cancer Society, 1988.

"Eating, Drinking and Associated Difficulties." Northampton, U.K.: Motor Neurone Disease Association, 1986.

"Specialty Food Shop Catalogue." Toronto, Ont.: Carecor Health Services Inc., annual.

"Eating and Swallowing in ALS: Patient Information," Carolyne Van Gool and Janet McEvoy. London, Ont.: University Hospital, 1989. Unpublished manuscript.

"Non-chew Cookbook," J.R. Wilson. Ottawa, Ont.: Canadian Hospital Association, 1988.

13

Breathing Strategies

The Process of Breathing

Normal "easy" breathing involves two main muscle groups (see figure). When you breathe in, the diaphragm moves down; at the same time, the intercostal muscles between your ribs contract to pull your rib cage up and out. These two actions cause a partial vacuum. Fresh air rushes down the windpipe, through the bronchi, which are the largest air passages in your lungs, and then into the small air sacs which pass fresh oxygen to the blood. This process is called "inspiration."

When you breathe out, both diaphragm and intercostal muscles relax; this decreases the size of your chest cavity. Used air, which contains waste carbon dioxide is pushed out of your lungs; this is "expiration."

If you are breathing heavily, two additional muscle groups come into play. When you take a deep breath in, muscles in the neck attached to the collarbone and upper ribs assist in breathing. When you force a breath out, your abdominal muscles help to push up the diaphragm.

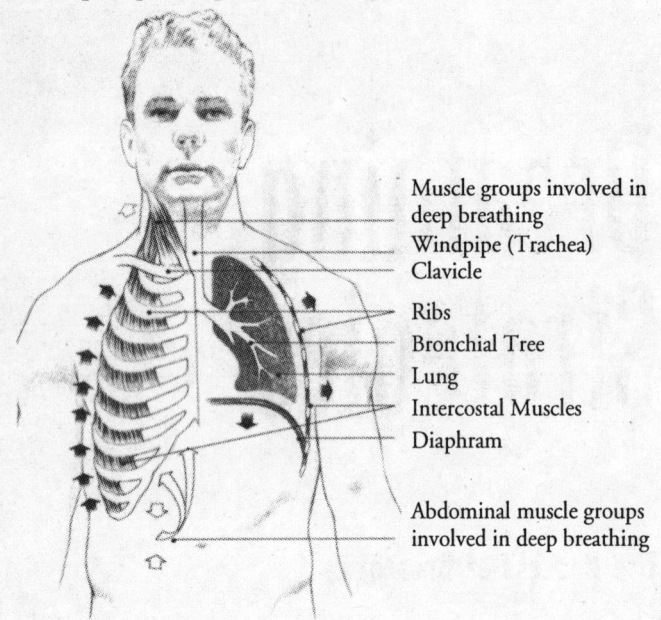

Muscle groups involved in deep breathing

Windpipe (Trachea)

Clavicle

Ribs

Bronchial Tree

Lung

Intercostal Muscles

Diaphram

Abdominal muscle groups involved in deep breathing

Cross-sectional view of the main air passages showing the four muscle groups involved in breathing: diaphram, intercostal, neck and abdomen.

ALS And Breathing

Breathing is largely an "involuntary" activity, although you can voluntarily change the speed or depth of your breathing. As the muscles involved in breathing are affected, you will experience decreased endurance and tire more easily, but it is important to know that these changes take place slowly. It is common for ALS patients to develop lung damage.

Two Simple Strategies

There are some straightforward steps you can take to help maintain your lung capacity and make breathing as easy as possible.

- Deep breathing exercise. This can be done twice a day. Slowly take a deep breath, hold it for two seconds and then exhale. This simple exercise will not reverse the progress of muscle weakening but it will help you to maintain lung capacity and muscle elasticity. Some doctors believe that patients who do deep breathing exercises are less prone to lung infections and partial lung collapse. Ask your physiotherapist to demonstrate an exercise routine and advise you about the use of exercise devices.
- Stop smoking. In addition to all the other problems smoking causes, it reduces lung capacity. It can also cause increased phlegm, which some patients will have difficulty clearing from their airways.

Pulmonary Function Testing

ALS affects breathing gradually. Pulmonary function testing is a way for your doctor to determine just how much your breathing is impaired. A series of painless tests will measure the effectiveness of your breathing. Inspiratory/expiratory pressure testing determines the strength of the muscles involved in breathing; the forced vital capacity test tells how much air you can move through your air passages in one breath; maximum breathing capacity tests measure how much air you can quickly move in and out of your lungs in a fixed time; air flow tests examine how smoothly air moves through your airway.

Symptoms of Breathing Impairment

Fatigue

Fatigue is a common symptom of ALS and is caused by a number of factors:

- As ALS attacks some of your motor neurons, they become unable to send commands from your brain to the muscle cells they control. So a smaller number of muscle cells must then try to perform jobs usually done by the full number. The result is that your muscles tire before they normally would.

- As your respiratory muscles are affected by the disease, they are able to draw less air into your lungs. When activity increases, it becomes more difficult for the lungs to supply enough oxygen to the body. Other metabolic changes take place and you feel fatigued.

- ALS produces many changes in your life. Change often results in general stress, which can manifest itself as fatigue. Don't let yourself become fatigued. Rest when you begin to feel tired. Try to keep your exertions within the limits your body is now imposing. Pay attention to signals like fatigue; it may be necessary to change your priorities and forego less important activities. Plan your day to include regular rest periods.

Morning Fatigue

Some persons with ALS also experience "morning fatigue"; they wake up feeling tired, sometimes with a headache and the feeling that they slept poorly. This may be caused by a weakness in the diaphragm. When you stand upright, the diaphragm moves down as you breathe in. When you lie down, the organs in your abdomen press against the diaphragm and more strength is required for the diaphragm to move down during breathing. So you may breathe less effectively at night if you are lying flat.

To help cope with this problem you should try to raise your head and shoulders during sleep. You can accomplish this by using two or more pillows under your head and shoulders, by choosing a wedge-shaped pillow or by raising the head of your bed on blocks four to six inches high.

Shortness of Breath with Activity

This may be the first symptom of weakening of breathing muscles. You may notice shortness of breath after rushing up stairs, carrying a load, etc. Shortness of breath can also occur with no particular exertion; you may not be able to walk or talk for long without becoming winded. You should tell your doctor about these symptoms. When you experience shortness of breath, stop what you are doing. Shortness of breath will disappear when activity is reduced. Relax in one of these positions if you are able; breathe slowly and deeply.

- Sit at a table, lean forward with a straight back and rest your head and shoulders on a pillow on the table.
- Sit on a chair or the edge of your bed; lean forward, keep your back straight and rest your elbows and forearms on your thighs.
- Lean against a wall with your feet about twelve inches from the wall. Rest your lower back against the wall and lean your upper back away from the wall.

Weak Cough

When you cough, your stomach muscles and intercostal muscles (between the ribs) contract quickly. This forces air from the lungs and up the airway; any mucus or food in the air passages is forced out as well. People with ALS have normal cough reflexes, but the muscles may be weakened and unable to produce a strong cough. You can strengthen your cough by a technique known as splinting the abdomen.

First take a deep breath, then clasp your arms firmly across your lower abdomen and bend over a high-back chair. Just as you cough out, squeeze your arms in tightly so that you push your abdomen in and down. It is important to time the bending and squeezing to coincide with the "expelling" phase of your cough. A variation on the self-assisted cough can be performed while sitting on a hard surface; clasp your arms over your abdomen and as you are about to cough out, bend forward quickly and squeeze the abdomen in and down.

If your arms are too weak to perform this manoeuvre, ask someone to help by pressing your forearms firmly into your abdomen, bending you forward as you cough. Ask your health-care professional to assist you and your helper to perfect this technique.

Excess Mucus and Secretions

In some patients, excess mucus and secretions can build up to the point where they cannot be easily cleared by coughing. This is particularly the case in early morning when secretions have built up all night. If you experience this problem, ask your physiotherapist to instruct you in methods to loosen secretions and bring them to the mouth to be spat out.

One method of dealing with mucus and saliva buildup is suctioning. Suction equipment acts very much like a dentist's suction tube; it consists of a motor, collection bottle, tubing and equipment; he or she will be able to tell you or your helper where to get the equipment and how to use it properly.

Respiratory Diseases

It is a good idea to avoid people who have colds or flu if you can. People with ALS are no more likely to catch these infections than other people, but they are more at risk of simple respiratory infections developing into pneumonia. Swallowing problems can cause food or drink to "go down the wrong way" into the lungs; this can irritate the lungs and cause pneumonia. (Chapter 12 discusses ways to avoid aspiration of food.)

If you do get a fever with bloody mucus coughed from the chest, or if you notice that the mucus has changed from clear white to yellowish, tell your doctor immediately; these could be symptoms of a respiratory infection that could lead to pneumonia.

Emergency Choking and Breathing Problems

The risk of choking while eating or drinking can be greatly reduced by use of the suggestions on diet and eating in Chapter 12. If you have problems with a weak cough, you or a helper can strengthen your cough by "splinting the abdomen."

If the airway is blocked by food or other obstruction, the assisted cough technique is not enough. You can tell when a person's airway is blocked: they cannot speak, appear to panic and signal choking with the hands on the throat. The Heimlich manoeuvre is the correct response to this type of emergency.

The helper stands behind the affected person and quickly and forcefully squeezes the abdomen with the fists. This is designed to dislodge the food or other obstruction from the air passage. To avoid possible injuries to the patient, it is a good idea for your family members or helpers to receive proper training in the Heimlich manoeuvre from a doctor, nurse or other health professional. The Heimlich manoeuvre and cardiopulmonary resuscitation (CPR) are useful skills for everyone to learn. Classes are available in most communities. Learning these techniques builds confidence for family and caregivers.

Direct Aids to Breathing

Failure of the respiratory muscles is an eventual result of ALS. Modern medical technology can offer portable life-support equipment, but the choice to use such equipment will have important consequences for your way of life and that of your family.

Ventilators are "controlling" devices that take over your breathing. The decision whether or not to use a ventilator is yours, but it is a decision you should make only after consulting with your family, your doctor and other health-care workers. Your doctor can tell you that you need a respirator; only you can decide if you want one. You will have to decide whether you are willing to accommodate your life and that of your family to dependence on a respirator. Can you count upon the assistance of family members, including a primary helper? It is important to remember that recent technology has produced portable, lightweight ventilators which allow considerable mobility, including travel. You should discuss the options available with both your medical practitioners and your family. If at all possible, the decision about a respirator should be made in a thoughtful way before a respiratory emergency develops, and you should ensure that your family is aware of your decision in case an emergency occurs. If you do decide that you are interested in ventilation, you will need to be referred to a respirologist.

Further Reading

"ALS: Strategies for Living." Vancouver, B.C.; ALS Society of British Columbia, 1989.

"Breathing in ALS; Patient Information," Anna Gallie and Karen Findlater. London, Ont.: ALS Support Team, University Hospital, 1989. Unpublished manuscript.

"Eating Drinking and Swallowing Strategies." Toronto, Ont.: ALS Society of Canada/ALS Society of Ontario, 1990.

14

How Can I Help?

A Guide for Family and Friends

It is important for family and friends to be aware of some of the feelings that a person with ALS will experience, and to bear with the expression of those feelings. You must try to accept and tolerate initial anger and sorrow, knowing that these are stages that will pass. Anger that seems to be directed at you is just the explosion of pent-up frustration. Try not to overreact. Your support may not seem to be helpful at the moment, but the knowledge that you are there to help is very important to the person with ALS.

Your own reaction to the diagnosis will of course depend upon how close you are to the person with ALS. For a family member or close friend, the news can be very traumatic. You may experience some of the feelings of denial, anger and depression already described. In addition, you may feel guilty—"Why him instead of me?" And there may be some resentment toward the person with ALS as you realize how your own life will be changed by the amount of work that will eventually be needed. These are all perfectly normal emotions, and you should not be hard on yourself for feeling them. There will be a transition period for you, too, as you learn to come to terms with ALS in someone you love.

Psychological Support

Acceptance of the disease does not mean giving up. It should be the first step in making the most of life with ALS. There is much that can be done to help the person with ALS continue to live a productive and enjoyable life. As a family member or friend, you will be able to help in many practical ways, but your psychological support may well be your most important contribution. Be positive, but do not trivialize the situation. It is foolish to pretend that everything will be fine, or that ALS is not a very serious condition. The person with ALS knows better and will "filter out" your comments if they are false. You will have decreased your ability to provide support.

On the other hand, there is no need to dwell on an overly pessimistic outlook. It is true that 20 percent of people with ALS live more than five years and that nearly 10 percent live ten years or more. It is also true that neurological research moves steadily ahead, and that no one can know when a breakthrough may appear. These facts give hope, and hope is a crucial part of life. Family and friends of people with ALS must try to achieve a correct balance between hope and realism. It is not an easy task.

For some people with ALS and their families, a minister, rabbi or priest can be a real source of strength. So can your local ALS chapter, which is dedicated to helping people with ALS and their families to cope with the disease. You can find out about your nearest local chapter by calling the ALS Society of Canada or your provincial society. If there is no local chapter near you, the Society will be able to refer you to another support group.

The Importance of Communication

Keeping the lines of communication open is an important part of the support you offer. People with ALS must know that they can always voice their feelings to a sympathetic listener who will not pass judgment on them. If you react with hurt feelings or try to belittle their fears, they will soon learn to keep their feelings to themselves. Perhaps your most important role is that of the good listener. The entire family should try to maintain an atmosphere in which all members can honestly express their own feelings about ALS.

Children of People with ALS

Although ALS is not primarily a disease of the young, it sometimes happens that the family of the person with ALS includes young children. It is easy to forget that they need to know how the disease will affect a loved parent and the whole family. It is important that family members and the counsellors helping the family take time to work through the problems children may have in coming to terms with ALS in their family.

Don't Forget About You

If you are a member of the immediate family, it is likely that you will become involved in the daily care and assistance of your person with ALS. Most ALSers remain in the home for as long as possible, and the demands upon members of the family can be great. Primary caregivers, such as spouses or grown children, may find that the care of the person with later-stage ALS is taking up most of their lives. It is natural to want to give all you can to help someone you love, but there should be limits to self-sacrifice.

When a vigorous person who is used to being in control of life is struck by a debilitating illness, he or she may react by transferring the desire for control onto others. Some people with ALS can become too demanding, and it is easy for family members to allow themselves to be controlled in this way. If you believe that this is happening to you, it is very important that you and the person with ALS discuss the situation and mutually agree on reasonable limits to your availability. If you cannot come to an agreement, it may be necessary for you to discuss your problem with a social worker or psychologist.

Caregivers must continue to have lives of their own. Time in the company of friends or family who are not sick, or in the pursuit of hobbies or activities besides caregiving, are important "refreshers." They allow you to recover from the stresses of caregiving and make you a better, more cheerful helper. Do not hesitate to ask other family members to fill in for you while you take regular breaks, or, if necessary, arrange for paid help to cover for you. The social worker who is part of the ALS medical team will be able to tell you about what types of help and what funding arrangements are available.

Practical Assistance

Personal Hygiene
Bathing and washing can continue with little modification in the early stages of ALS. Special tape or decals on the bottom of the tub will help prevent slipping, and a handrail at the

side of the tub is useful when entering or leaving. Later, a bath-bench may be helpful, and it may be necessary for you to help the person with ALS get into and out of the tub. As with all helping techniques that involve lifting, get proper training from the physiotherapist so you do not strain yourself. In the later stages of the disease, a bed-bath may be the best method, and the person with ALS should be encouraged to do as much of the bath as possible. Both of you can be trained in the proper technique by the nurse.

It is a good idea for a person with ALS to keep fingernails and hair short—and fashionable, too! If a woman (or a man) uses hair colouring, there is no reason to discontinue the practice. Hand-held shower sprays can be a great help in hair-washing. It is important that personal hygiene and grooming habits be maintained as much as possible. Knowing that you look your best is a great morale booster. Encourage your person with ALS by noticing and complimenting his or her appearance just as you have done in the past. Be there to help if necessary but do not undermine independence and privacy when you are not needed.

Activity and Recreation

In the early stages of ALS there may be little need to modify the usual recreational activities. People with ALS are encouraged to be as active as their strength allows, but they must not become over-fatigued. Fatigue will rob them of the energy they need to take part in the activities they really enjoy or really need to perform.

A cane or walker will allow continued mobility for those with weakness in the legs. Eventually a wheelchair may be required. It is important that a wheelchair be properly prescribed. There are many models available, some with very helpful attachments. To ensure that a wheelchair serves the person with ALS for the longest possible time, seek the expertise of the occupational therapist; he or she will know which model is the best purchase for your person with ALS. The therapist can also train you to help in transfers from wheelchair to car, wheelchair to stationary chair and wheelchair to bed.

Outings are good morale-boosters; everyone can benefit from a change of scene and a break in routine. Many public facilities, such as art galleries, museums and theatres, are wheelchair accessible, as are many restaurants. Encourage your person with ALS to get out, and be available as a companion.

For people with ALS who have limited mobility and muscle weaknesses, there are still many recreational activities available that can be shared with family and friends. Cards, chess and other board games are enjoyable social activities, and there are card trays available for those with grasping problems. People with ALS can paint, write books and garden, using supportive devices and equipment if necessary. Being together and watching TV or listening to radio, stereo or talking books (available at public libraries) are other alternatives. Reading aloud in a group was an activity much practised by our Victorian forebears, and it can make a nice change from TV. A recreation therapist will have many suggestions about other possible activities.

Whatever the chosen activities, the important element is that they are shared. ALS can lead to a sense of isolation. The best help that family and friends can offer is their company, their ability to listen, their loving inclusion of the person with ALS in family and group activities wherever possible, their assistance when it is needed and their tact in knowing when it is not.

Where to Go For Help

At the national level, the ALS Society of Canada provides support, direction and initiatives to find the cause of ALS.

Their activities include:
- support of medical research
- fundraising
- public awareness
- development of educational materials
- providing information on current research in newsletters for the general public and the medical profession
- providing support for assistive devices and equipment required by people with ALS (in conjunction with the Muscular Dystrophy Association of Canada)

For more information call or write:

ALS SOCIETY OF CANADA
90 Adelaide Street East, Suite B101
Toronto, Ontario M5C 2R4

In addition, all across the country there is a network of provincial societies under the umbrella of the ALS Society of Canada. As part of this national team, your provincial society has declared its mandate:
- to eliminate ALS;
- to enhance the quality of life of patients and family;
- to educate the general public and health professionals.

Your provincial society offers:
- local chapters and peer support;
- Basic Information Series on ALS (a series of booklets on life strategies for day-to-day living with ALS);
- referral services.

Please register with your provincial society for more information, direction and support.

Further Reading

"ALS: Strategies for Living." Vancouver, B.C.: ALS Society of B.C., 1989.

Further Reading (continued)

"Basic Home Care for ALS Patients." Woodland Hills, CA: The ALS Association, 1989.

"Breathing Strategies." Toronto, Ont.: ALS Society of Canada/ALS Society of Ontario, 1990.

"Care of the Patient with Amyotrophic Lateral Sclerosis," by the Group of ALS Support Personnel (GRASP) University Hospital, London, Ontario. Toronto, Ont.: ALS Society of Canada.

"Communication Strategies." Toronto, Ont.: ALS Society of Canada/ALS Society of Ontario, 1990.

"Eating, Drinking and Swallowing Strategies." Toronto, Ont.: ALS Society of Canada/ALS Society of Ontario, 1990.

"Help Yourself! Hints from the Handicapped." Ottawa, Ont.: Health and Welfare Canada, 1984.

"Home Health Care," Jo-Ann Friedman. New York, N.Y.: Norton, 1986.

"Home Management of Motor Neurone Disease." Northampton, U.K.: Motor Neurone Disease Association.

"Living with Motor Neurone Disease." Northampton, U.K.: Motor Neurone Disease Association.

"Meeting the Challenge of Disability or Chronic Illness—A Family Guide." Baltimore, MD: Paul H. Brookes Publishing Co., 1986.

"Mobility Strategies." Toronto, Ont.: ALS Society of Canada/ALS Society of Ontario, 1990.

"Nursing a Loved One at Home," Susan Goldman. Philadelphia, PA: Running Press Book Publishers, 1988.

Part Three

The Provocative Stuff

You can drop me in the ocean

You can plant me in the ground

Pop me in the oven and then sprinkle me around

Offer me in sacrifice

Burn me at the stake

Just don't play Leonard Cohen at my wake

I'm lying in bed.
Glistening beads of sweat have
formed on my brow.
My chest is heaving.
Above me, quivering with anticipation,
is the focus of all my concentration.
With one swift penetrating plunge,
a flood of hot fluid rushes
to the surface and finally,
in a heap of spent flesh,
I surrender.
One more satisfied mosquito
has had its way with me.

15

I've Fallen and I Can't Get Up

There's a very fine line between sparking discussion and igniting anger. If this chapter results in the latter, as a writer, I will have to consider myself a failure.

Just before you die, your whole life is supposed to flash before your eyes. ALS doesn't take you as suddenly as a car crash, which might explain why my life seems to have been passing before me in slow motion. It's true. It feels like a lifetime since D-Day, and my outlook now is nothing like it was in the beginning. I'll probably never remember, with any clarity, the flood of images that bombarded my psyche that day, but the way I've got it figured there's a perfectly good reason for this. Only through a kind of self-imposed amnesia could I provide the mental climate necessary for denial to flourish. It's as if, to better deal with the severity of the doctor's diagnosis, my thoughts were placed in a sort of psychic suspension. I'm not a psychologist, but I am convinced that denial plays an important role in our ability to absorb trauma. None of us gets to practise dying, so it stands to reason we would have some form of natural defence against nervous breakdown. If this weren't the case, we'd probably croak just from hearing the bad news.

So denial may be helpful, but of course all good neuroses have to come to an end. You can only watch yourself deteriorate for so long before your avoidance of the truth must give way to truth itself. For me it lasted about a year. Once I started to accept the reality of my situation, an amazing transition began. You see, emotion is like steam. Eventually, if you let it build up long enough, it's bound to explode. And just as denial helps control a sudden rise in emotion, acceptance, providing it's gradual, controls the release of those same emotions. This acceptance is what I call my personal pressure-relief valve. Over time, the fears I suppressed on D-Day have come to the surface, and thanks to this relief valve, they have surfaced gently enough for me to comprehend.

One of the first fears to return was also one of the worst. For a time, an almost indescribable pain came over me whenever I looked into the eyes of my children. How dark times must have been when men only took pride in sons. Rebecca, our first-born daughter, was only six, and the excitement of starting school was the most important thing in her world. But that first day, watching the school bus pull up brought only melancholy. I wouldn't see her excited and filled with butterflies before the first big school play. I wouldn't hear the shrieks and giggles of her first pyjama party. As she got on the bus, I watched her tiny hand waving, but all I could think of was the graduation I'd never see.

Our youngest daughter, Michalla, wasn't even two yet, and I couldn't help thinking I would run out of time before we even got to know each other. Nothing I'd learned to this point in my life could prepare me for feelings like these. But I did see that school play. And it was so noisy at Rebecca's first pyjama party that I got to yell "Keep it down!" just like a real Dad. Michalla and I not only got to know each other, I saw *her* first school play, too. She played the lead role in the widely acclaimed grade one production of "Little Red Hen." As for graduations, it's unlikely, but I don't rule anything out any more. What I do rule out is wallowing in self-pity. I may not be able to teach my kids how best to row against the tide or show them the breathtaking awe of a wilderness sunrise, but by maintaining my spirit I believe I can teach them something equally valuable, something they can use for the rest of their lives.

Another early fear was admittedly vain, perhaps macho, but it was an undeniable and integral part of the condition. It was the impending loss of physical prowess. I was never what you'd consider a Charles Atlas, but it's safe to say that neither muscle nor stamina were things I needed more of. I never thought about it much back then, but upon reflection, I derive a kind of blue-collar pride from the fact that my fitness was the result not of working out, but of working. If I'd been a rocket scientist, or even a high school graduate, things might have been different, but I wasn't. Seven days a week, I managed a twenty-four-hour marine freight service. Because I did this almost single-handedly, fulfilling my role as sole bread-winner was dependent on perfect health. If I could no longer provide for my family, how long could I go on masquerading as a husband and father? If I really was bound for physical ruin, how long could I cling to the notion of masculinity? Day-to-day deterioration only fuelled feelings of inadequacy, and for a while, self-esteem fell to an all-time low.

What a fool, eh? There I was, facing the most serious challenge of my life, and I couldn't see past my own pectorals.

Instead of acknowledging the real threat (the threat to my sanity), I was basing my entire sense of personal worth on some Neanderthal definition of manhood. After all, I'd managed to get to that point in my life with virtually no hair on my chest. I didn't drag my knuckles when I walked. Muscles weren't my problem. The problem was my reverence for them. If I had kept up that line of reasoning, eventually I wouldn't have needed ALS…I could have just depressed myself to death.

Thank goodness the measure of a man isn't in how much he can hold above his head. I'm coming to believe that our true measure involves the things we can't hold at all. I couldn't touch depression, but I learned to control it. I couldn't touch anger, either, but I learned to control that too. I still get mad at the little things—like when they play "Achey Breaky Heart" more than once in the same solar system—but ALS-related anger has become a thing of the past.

Today I measure my strength, or lack of it, in terms of my ability to control things like resentment and frustration. I'm convinced these two emotions, all by themselves, have the potential to destroy a person. Despite my best efforts, I still can't help resenting the burden I've become. I've managed to forgive people I never thought I'd forgive, but I can't seem to forgive ALS for dragging my loved ones into my all-consuming situation. Each and every thing I accomplish is, in one way or another, directly related to the labour of others, and ironically, it's almost exclusively the labour of those same people I most wanted to provide for. Even my folks would be denied the son that would have been there to help them through their old age. I'm still working on it, but as of right now, I'm afraid the score stands at: resentment—one; Dennis—nothing.

Last, but not least, there's frustration. Recently, a television reporter asked me what the most frustrating thing was about having a disease like ALS. Even though talking is extremely difficult, I'm seldom at a loss for barely intelligible words; however, this particular question left me temporarily speechless. After a long, uncomfortable pause, the best I could do was mumble some flippant remark like, "Have you got a couple days?" We eventually finished the interview, but for several days after, his question kept replaying itself over and over like a tape loop in the back of my mind. I've come to believe that there is no clear-cut answer.

Had I been asked the same question in the first year, I quite likely would have pinned my frustration on institutional double-talk and government red tape. A couple years later, it probably would have been falling—falling down stairs, falling up stairs, falling off chairs, falling out of bed, falling, falling everywhere. I even considered having someone put a "Watch For Falling ALSers" sign at the top of our driveway. It wouldn't have been so bad if I'd been able to get up, but once I went down I just writhed around like a wounded bug until someone got home. Then I'd catch supreme shit for wobbling around when I'd promised not to. For a while we had a (pardon the pun) standing joke around our place. It was my repeated request that decent reading material be stapled to the ceiling. I'll be the first to admit that long periods of time staring up from cold linoleum tends to have a frustrating effect, but one or two stimulating articles, perhaps even the odd well-placed girly picture, could have made a world of difference.

A year or so later, my biggest frustration would have been my deteriorating speech. Make no mistake, it's definitely frustrating when new clients assume you've been drinking and ever so politely put you on perpetual hold. The main reason behind my speech loss was a falling palate, which meant that whenever I tipped my head too far forward, any fluid in my mouth was automatically channelled around and out my nose—milk, coffee, saliva...whatever. You simply haven't lived till you've experienced the eye-watering thrill of a Listerine head douche. No kidding—if you were to put your mouth over mine, pinch my nose and exhale, you could quite literally blow my mind!

Speaking of having your mind blown, it's all kind of foggy now, but during that brief lapse of sanity when I decided to start my video production business, I got a super-deluxe, state-of-the-art, thump-your-brains-out sound system. Ruth can still crank it up, but I can't dance. This is frustrating. My mind still gets going like the Barenaked Ladies on PCP, but the rest of me just sways around precariously like Rita MacNeil on a double-dose of Demerol. Sure, if I hold my tongue just right I can keep time with my toes, but somehow, wiggling one's appendages to the likes of Jeff Healey or Powder Blues just doesn't cut the musical mustard.

You want frustration? I'll give you frustration. Frustration is watching a baby-faced teenager pull on an NHL jersey and net enough in his first season to single-handedly finance Canada's entire ALS research program.

You want frustration? I'll give you frustration. Frustration smoulders in Canada's National Art Gallery: three stripes of publicly funded obscenity called *Voice of Fire;* a $1.7-million epitaph to our psychotic sense of priority. And as if to rub salt in my wounded sensibility, as I type these words, the same gallery has just approved the purchase of an equally lifeless piece of elitist excrement, this time for a paltry $1.8 million. It's probably a foolish notion, but sometime between splatters, maybe one of these abstractionist con artists could accidentally kick over a pail of paint and donate a chunk of their floor to the ALS Society.

What is the most frustrating thing about having ALS? In the past I could easily have rattled off a long list of things, but today the answer to that reporter's question is gradually losing its importance. What's far more important is whether or not relating my frustrations to others will result in any tangible difference.

As I continue my reluctant slide toward complete muscular coma, my skeleton-like appearance leaves me able to draw polite sympathy, but the tangible difference I'm really talking about is going to require the education of able-bodied people everywhere. It must be universally understood that ALS is not just a disease with no cure, and it's not just a disease with no treatment. ALS, after 125 years, is a disease with no known cause. It must be universally understood that ALS kills more people annually than many higher-profile conditions combined. Every debilitating disease is a tragedy in its own right, so this isn't to suggest, in any way, that other diseases are insignificant. I am suggesting, however, that the abysmal state of ALS awareness, in particular, is inadvertently a declaration of our insignificance.

Statistically, I'm beginning to see the lack of ALS awareness as symptomatic of another kind of sickness, a bureaucratic malignancy in the very heart of our health-care system. I want to believe I matter as much as the next person, but it has become impossible to ignore the numbers, and unfortunately, it has also become impossible to separate public awareness from public opinion. Public opinion, all too often, swings like a pendulum between the predictable politics of media and the petty politics of government. The most glaring example of this pendulum is evident in today's AIDS issue.

If I didn't think there were important lessons to be learned, I wouldn't bother treading on such controversial quicksand, but somehow AIDS awareness has become the standard by which hundreds of other charities must now measure themselves. Can you remember the last time you heard or read the words Acquired Immune Deficiency Syndrome? More to the point, can you remember a day when you didn't? Unless you've been living in a cave, you know who gets it. You know how it's transmitted. You probably know a great many things about AIDS. But did you also know that in Canada, in the past ten years, the death toll for AIDS and ALS is virtually identical? In barely a decade, North Americans have not only learned how to avoid getting AIDS, they have allocated well over $3 billion (that's $3,000,000,000) to fight it. And yet, after a century and a quarter, the average person doesn't know what ALS stands for, let alone what it is. I'm sorry, but that is frustrating!

This particular form of frustration has literally split my conscience in two. It's like I've become a sort of social schizophrenic—torn between the part of me that's living and the part of me that's dying. The living me admires AIDS lobbyists for their organization, their dedication and especially for their tenacity. But the dying me envies them for their power and the ease with which they tap the mainstream media. The living me wants to stand up and applaud their unprecedented success, but the dying me can't overlook the disparity such instant success represents. The living me is ashamed of feelings like these, but after several years of hearing the same frustration echoed among health-care workers and other shut-ins, the dying me would be even more ashamed to leave these words unsaid.

You see, when John or Jane Doe reads another newspaper article on AIDS the effect is fleeting, but when those in terminal circles see another newspaper story, or magazine article, or billboard, or public service announcement, or openline radio program, or television talk show, or special news feature, or made-for-TV movie, or Act-Up protester screaming about how AIDS is being ignored, many of us wince with a kind of pain only the dying can understand. I'm still learning how to wrap that pain in a nice, neat, politically correct package, so what I say next will no doubt be seen as incompatible with the agendas of extremists on both sides.

Even though more than 90 percent of the world's AIDS cases are heterosexual, an all-too-willing western press continues to maintain an indivisible marriage between AIDS and gay rights. Based on my longest friendship, and on people I've worked with, I firmly believe the vast majority of gays to be kind-hearted, fair-minded individuals with the same goals and aspirations as everyone else—nothing like the Act-Up fanatics who claim to represent them. Somehow it must be conveyed that many so-called homophobics would more readily embrace the civil rights struggle if only they were allowed to divorce the two issues. In other words, if those same people didn't draw their conclusions from the six o'clock news, they'd be less apt to perceive gays in general as shrill, obnoxious flakes who don't give a shit about anyone but themselves. If it can somehow be accepted that there are many whose frustration is often compounded by this kind of genuine confusion, then it can also be accepted that a fundamental question needs to be answered. Where do those of us who are truly being ignored direct our frustration? At the fringe groups for milking such a destructive myth, the media for perpetuating it, or the entire homosexual community for allowing itself to be sold so aggressively as synonymous with a single disease? I just don't know what to think any more.

Perhaps the best way to put these feelings in perspective is by analogy. Picture a long line of sickly, emaciated people outside a disaster relief shelter. Inside the shelter an army of volunteers works feverishly to keep up, only instead of handing out clothing and bowls of gruel, every so often someone's name is called and they're handed a life-saving pill. Many lack the strength to stand. Some have cancer. Others have failing hearts. Down the line there are people with everything from incurable motor disorders to inoperable brain tumours. All have grief-stricken loved ones. All are starving for cures. All are dying. Suddenly, out of nowhere, a newcomer barges his way to the front of the line and starts shrieking at the volunteers, "Hey, you in there, can't you see I'm dying? Where's my pill? What's the hold-up? Come on, I haven't got all day!"

The point being, death has no sexual preference, and no amount of yelling, screaming or spitting on politicians will ever change that. Radicals aren't to blame. They just aren't entitled to lay blame while reaping the benefits of the most responsive, expensive and concerted research effort in history. In the meantime, the ongoing orgy of gratuitous sound-bites will probably continue. Whoever yells the loudest and on cue will continue to absorb the lion's share of financial support, and those too weak to move or yell at all will continue to grovel for spare change. With a few saintly exceptions, journalists will continue fellating those who promise the most controversy, politicians will continue pandering to whichever issues make prime time, and people dying of plain old diseases like ALS will continue to go comparatively unnoticed. It just seems to be the way things are.

CBC "Morningside"

Dear Peter,

I know I said that I'd probably be history by now, and to be completely honest, I really didn't think I'd be writing the CBC again, but it's getting so you can't depend on anything anymore. I thought that maybe I would die last spring but I just haven't been able to find the time. Take this morning for example; the alarm went off and before you could say Amyotrophic Lateral Sclerosis, my eyes were open again. It's a good thing too because I need them open to use some of the new gadgets I have.

Enter…my automatic page flipper; a sophisticated tool specifically designed to turn the pages of a book. And I used to think the space shuttle was advanced. Through a series of intricate guides, rollers and page holders, this moving mass of mechanical ingenuity successfully duplicates the dexterity of the human hand. It took no time to master and in fact, I just finished reading the latest edition of Morningside

Papers, which by the way lay unconscionably unread since last Christmas. Being able to read again is, in every sense of the word, a gift. Nonetheless, after spending so much of my working life at physically demanding jobs, I still find it incredible that I could so quickly be reduced to needing a machine just to move a piece of paper. Irregardless, when I couple mechanical godsends like these to the mobility that an electric wheelchair offers, life remains well worth living.

In fact, I have a whole new theory on life. The loss of an arm or leg often results in a transfer of strength to the remaining limbs and they say that when you lose your sight or hearing, your remaining senses somehow become heightened. Similarly, when you have A.L.S. and you're robbed of the ability to do anything, you gain the ability to appreciate everything.

A friend of ours named Graham died recently, leaving a wife and two young children. Like me, he was only in his thirties. The disease struck him with its usual merciless severity, taking him in just three years. On average, A.L.S. has run its course and killed its victim in two and a half years so I began to think that I, well into my fifth year, had been singled out for cruel and unusual punishment. I had even begun to look upon Graham's death, in secret, as a luxury that I was being denied. I could not have been more wrong. Unlike me, Graham and thousands like him have been taken so swiftly that there simply isn't time to adjust. The disease's spread is normally so rapid that for most A.L.S.ers and their families, just coping becomes all-consuming.

I suppose a similar outcome awaits me too but because the disease in my case has been slightly more lenient, I'm better able to absorb what is happening to me. If I am being granted time to face my own disintegration, squandering that time would be nothing less than an insult to people like Graham who fought so hard.

Geese have begun their long flight south and as western leaves show their first signs of changing colour it looks like I'm about to see another autumn. How long I hang around has become irrelevant. The important thing is, I'm actually looking forward to another spring.

Sincerely yours,

The Incredible Shrinking Man

No agitation; no media coverage.

No media coverage; no public awareness.

No public awareness; no funding.

No funding; no cure.

16

First We Take Vancouver

If you haven't already figured it out, I'm pretty high on public awareness. I firmly believe the absence of awareness to be the single biggest obstacle to our ever finding a cure for ALS. Admittedly, an unprecedented amount of attention has come our way recently as a result of the controversy surrounding assisted suicide, but I can only assume that when we lose Sue Rodriguez we'll once again be pushed off the edge of the media map.

You probably think I've said this often enough already, but for the benefit of those with short attention spans, I want to say it one more time. ALS is not rare! I don't mean to belittle, in any way, the severity of other conditions. But urn for urn, casket for casket, in the past decade ALS has killed as many

Canadians as AIDS, and continues to kill more Canadians annually than such well-known diseases as Multiple Sclerosis, Muscular Dystrophy, Cystic Fibrosis and Huntington's disease combined.

I can and have been accused of setting up a kind of hierarchy of disease with my comments on lifestyle-related illnesses. Elsewhere in the book I've alluded to smoking and cancer, when in truth I used to smoke like a house on fire. I've mentioned booze-induced liver problems, when anyone who knows me knows that often the only thing separating me from a stiff drink is my straw. And up until I settled down, I rarely said no to drugs or casual sex, so the last thing I want to do is come off sounding holier-than-thou. I could have contracted another disease, but I didn't. I have ALS, and I know of no better way to put its obscurity in perspective than by comparison.

When I was first diagnosed, Ruth and I hadn't even heard of ALS, and to begin with, I foolishly thought we were alone in our ignorance. But the more I investigated, the more I discovered that, in actuality, we were only part of an ignorance so pervasive and longstanding that, for a time, I let my bitterness get the upper hand. It soon became obvious, though, that bitterness would solve nothing, and that if researchers were ever to receive the funding they required, some fundamental change would have to take place. I still had a couple years to kill so I set out to change the world…at least that was the plan. Needless to say the world just kept spinning and I kept thinning—but along the way I did learn quite a bit about the way things work.

Because ALS awareness has traditionally been in the hands of non-profit charity organizations, I deliberated long and hard over whether or not to include the next few paragraphs. It's a troubling paradox. Even though I see how much is being done, each time I hear someone ask what ALS is, I'm reminded of how much isn't. There will no doubt be those who mistake my criticism for lack of gratitude, but one need only look around my house to see how much I have to be truly grateful for. I'm literally surrounded by charity-owned living aids, so I'm constantly reminded of the wonderful work these groups do. Nevertheless, when someone feels strongly enough on a given issue, he should be willing to go on record, even if by doing so he risks alienating some of his most powerful allies.

In Canada, there are two groups committed to ALS research and patient care. One is the Amyotrophic Lateral Sclerosis Society. The other is the older and much larger Muscular Dystrophy Association. The former concerns itself exclusively with ALS. The latter handles over forty diseases, one of which happens to be ALS. Each group has provincial chapters from coast to coast. Each group (at least in B.C.) is an invaluable source of practical support: wheelchairs, bathroom aids, stuff like that. Each group publishes stacks of informative pamphlets covering everything from diagnosis to rigor mortis. Each group can refer its members (especially those who live near city centres) to a broad range of professional therapists. And finally, each group would cease to exist were it not for the boundless spirit of countless volunteers.

I've been on the receiving end of both charities for several years, so I can say with some authority that from a client's point of view, each organization fills an identical role. The problem is, they're also identical in their approach to public awareness; neither one gives it even a modicum of priority.

The ALS Society of Canada, for example, devotes less than 5 percent of its annual budget to educate the general public, even though almost every cent they spend on medical research and on people like me is the direct result of public donation. The MDA is a bit different. They rely heavily on their well-known telethon but, oddly enough, openly prohibit the purchase of television air time. It's one thing to give something a low priority for budgetary reasons, but it's quite another to have an iron-clad policy against it, especially when that something is the most cost-effective means of mass communication known to human kind.

As I type these words, I'm closing in on my eighth year with ALS. For seven of those years I've tried my level best to convince the people with the purse strings that an ounce of public awareness is worth a pound of public support, but my point of view has not prevailed. Friends and family have raised several thousand dollars for the ALS cause. One friend raised money by walking in a gruelling trans-mountain trek from Gold River to Tahsis. Others took part in more traditional fundraisers like Cornflower Day. Teachers at our local elementary school even expanded their annual Terry Fox Fun Run to include pledges for ALS, and in the process (to the best of my knowledge) raised more per capita than any other community in Canada. But despite repeatedly making my feelings known, at every level, virtually none of the resulting donations were ever set aside for public awareness.

Enter "Bid For Change!" The idea was nothing original: I would auction off my photo collection and use the proceeds to broadcast a public service announcement on local television. The last few years have taught me that having a disease like ALS means accepting a kind of Catch-22. In this high-tech world of thirty second sound-bites and split-second imagery, raising awareness takes money, but the flipside is, raising that money takes awareness. People just don't give to causes they know nothing about. So the basic rationale behind "Bid For Change" was to provide a way for people who didn't know the first thing about ALS to give and also receive something tangible in return.

Before we knew it, more than fifty other artists had joined the effort and we were off to the races. It's safe to say that this auction taught me more about human nature than any other single event in my life. The months of preparation leading up to it were literally filled with lessons. One moment my ego was being stroked; the next moment my face was being slapped. It spawned new-found friendships, and although I won't go so far as to say it created any bona fide rivalries, there was definitely no shortage of people eager to jam sticks in my spokes.

The success of the project can be measured like this: in British Columbia, in 1991, a small army of dedicated Cornflower Day volunteers hit the streets and raised $42,000. By comparison, in 1992 (the year I made my bid for change), in one town, in one room, in one evening, one half-dead ALSer and a small band of supportive sidekicks took in a little over $20,000. I was convinced that raising half the amount usually attributed to an entire province would finally send a signal to the higher-ups, but the truth is, our efforts were never even acknowledged. I'm not sure what it's going to take to change the present executive mind-set, but I do know that until our hand-to-mouth budgetary policies are re-priorized in favour of awareness, we'll have no one to blame but ourselves.

CBC "Morningside"

Dear Peter,

They said things like "Dennis, it'll never work, art auctions have been done to death," "The timing's all wrong," "You'll be lucky to break even," and my personal favourite, "Dennis, you aren't following proper channels." Well, it would be juvenile of me to gloat on national radio, so instead, to all the nay-sayers, I offer these timeless words of profundity and wisdom...five words to be exact. Count 'em. Na na, na na na.

What a night! I felt like a skinny version of Kevin Costner in that baseball movie…"Hold an auction and they will come." The doors opened, a crowd filled the room, and two and a half hours later, poof, $20,000. It was one of those nights where everything that could go wrong didn't.

I have to admit, though, for a family of hicks from Quadra Island, we were a bit out of our element. The auction was held in one of those swanky conference centres where even the public washrooms have two-ply paper. If that's not enough, we were right next door to the Empress Hotel, a huge four-ply establishment right on Victoria's harbourfront. As a belated birthday gift, my dearheart of a mother booked us into one of their wheelchair-accessible rooms, so when the auction was over, and everyone went home, I just motored upstairs to a stiff nightcap and a soft bed.

But nightcap or not, long after Ruth and the girls nodded off, I lay awake unable to absorb an evening that had slipped by all too quickly. I thought of my new-found booty, and how I could finally buy a bit of TV time to spread the word. And I thought of the small but unstoppable circle of friends who helped me pull it off. Unfortunately, I couldn't help also thinking that in all the excitement, I had overlooked two glaring disappointments.

Understand that this fundraiser took place less than one block from the B.C. Legislature. Call me naive, but I really thought a venue in the heart of my provincial capital might attract one or two like-minded politicians. Invitations were printed, envelopes and stamps were purchased and the lick-athon began. What a waste of saliva! Despite inviting every city official, MLA and MP from Premier to town dog-catcher, not one (repeat) not one dignitary found my efforts to be worthy of their "honourable" presence.

Even more surprising, and especially disheartening, was an equally underwhelming response from the media. If it weren't for "Morningside" I'm sure I'd have given up long ago. After sending out no less than forty-six news releases, not a single reporter came to the auction. Not one! Again, you could call me naive, but considering some of the fluff that passes for journalism these days, I figured an event like "Bid For Change" should have rated a few seconds somewhere. Instead, I came home to panels of experts debating Fergie's up-to-the-minute mammary status, and endless reruns of the Woody Allen Libido Report. Surely, a few thousand dying Canadians deserve better.

(It should be noted that, as Great Britain's official ALS Patroness, Fergie's selfless and extensive efforts rarely made headlines. And believe it or not, up until the professional Peeping Toms of the British press started Sarah's public flogging, she had considered attending the auction.)

Finally, in my quest for sleep, I remember counting works of art like some folks count sheep. After all, how could I forget the artists? It was the artists (all fifty-two of them) whose talent and generosity personified what I've been trying to say all along: that people really will help if they're only made aware.

So you see on one hand, if I could, I'd pat myself on the back, but on the other hand, the collective yawn from news-meisters and bureaucrats tells me that in terms of true awareness, I haven't even scratched the surface. With one more unexpected summer behind me, ALS continues to deal me physical failure and defeat, but that night, if I'd been able to raise a glass and my voice to speak, I'd have made a simple toast…to big plans, bigger hearts, and most of all, to small victories.

Yours as always,
The Incredible Shrinking Man

In 1869, a French neurologist named Charcot first identified what's known today as Amyotrophic Lateral Sclerosis. A century and a quarter later, while Canada celebrates 125 years of progress, ALSers quietly look back on almost no progress at all.

There was a time when ALS enjoyed a great deal more publicity than it does today. Thanks to one famous athlete, for a while, decades ago, it was actually the focus of widespread media attention. I've come to admire and appreciate the achievements of Lou Gehrig, but with all due respect, time marches on, and today's youth simply don't know the "Ironman" from a hole in the ground. My children only know that their father has ALS. Almost daily, they're bombarded with slick television campaigns aimed at ridding the earth of everything from canine heartworms to feminine itch, but rarely a word about what's killing their Dad. Admittedly, one auction does not awareness make, but once the crowd gathered and the bidding began, my kids could clearly see that each of us, in our own way, really can make a difference.

A century and a quarter of under-publicized and underfunded research tells me that if we're ever to find a cure, we must look not to organizations but to individuals like the ones reading this book. If you'd like to contribute to a special fund dedicated to ALS awareness, and awareness alone, make your cheque or money order payable to:

ALS Awareness Foundation
P.O. Box 532,
Quathiaski Cove, B.C.
V0P 1N0

"Don't believe I'm taken in
by stories I have heard.
I just read the daily news
and swear by every word."

— Steely Dan

17

Princes and Thieves

If I were to lump all of my newspaper, radio and television interviews together, they would only total something less than twenty, so I'm definitely not an authority when it comes to the mechanics of media. However, I think I'd be remiss if I didn't pass on my limited knowledge to other aspiring awareness fanatics who may choose to walk a similar road. For the second time since starting this book, I'm genuinely torn between tempering my anger and letting fly…partly because media-bashing is already getting far too fashionable, but mostly because I've developed a couple close friendships within media circles, friendships I hate to jeopardize. So whether you see the following diatribe as the height of hypocrisy or simply passé, rest assured, not one word of it came easy.

Even though my wheelchair is powered, I can't reach the control without help, so once I get to where I'm going and flop my hand back into a comfortable position, I often spend long periods of time anchored to one spot. Consequently, television has become a much bigger part of my life than it otherwise would have been. You could say I've become the quintessential captive audience.

Anyway, a couple years back our landlord sold the house we were renting to some wealthy folks who needed a summer home, and we were forced to move out. We ended up in an aging but comfortable place on the other side of the island, and as luck would have it, planted outside on a rock bluff was a satellite dish. It was old and irreparably seized to its base, but it was still aimed at a satellite with quite a few channels. Suddenly having access to the heavens impacted my daily routine in a major way. The most I'd ever gotten before was one or two channels, so for a while I was like a kid in a candy store. Ruth and the girls took turns acting as my remote (I admit clicking them more often than I should have) and with their help I entered the information age.

Because I see awareness and media as inseparably linked, I quite naturally took a special interest in the way current affairs were being presented. This is a polite way of saying I turned into a bug-eyed news junkie. Sometimes I'd get out-voted, but most of the time, if I did my "I need the TV cuz I have ALS" sulk, I'd get the channel I wanted.

It isn't an exaggeration to say that, because of my stationary circumstance, I take in ten times more news than the average viewer. At my disposal was a veritable banquet of choices, and to begin with my appetite was insatiable. The problem was, the more I devoured, the more disenchanted and misinformed I felt. Eventually, I became so information-ally obese that no matter what part of the menu I chose from, everything tasted the same.

I realized early on that I had traditionally been viewing the news from a false perspective. I, as a consumer, believed journalism, as a profession, was somehow devoid of agenda—immune to the corruption it covered. Until my multi-channel initiation, I'd always been able to envision a day when ALS would find its rightful place in the loop, but as I pecked my days away, the continuous background sounds of political rhetoric, pre-packaged tragedy and celebrity scandal had a way of wearing down my optimism.

This was my frame of mind when the unthinkable finally happened. It was March 3, 1993, a little after nine in the evening, and I was tuned to the CBC's "Prime Time News." Ironically, I was working away on my public awareness chapter when I heard Pamela Wallin calmly say the words "genetic breakthrough." At first it barely caught my attention, but when she ended her sentence with the name Lou Gehrig, something quite literally snapped. I'm not trying to be cute. Something actually did snap. It was as if, for a split second, my body forgot it was broken, because my head jerked up so fast and so hard that I popped something out of kilter in my neck.

The collaborative efforts of researchers, primarily in Montreal and Boston, had resulted in the pinpointing of a key genetic defect. There's actually no hereditary connection in the vast majority of ALS cases, so I knew my excitement was premature. I also knew it would probably be years before this or any other discovery was likely to yield a cure. But that didn't stop me from savouring every last word. In less than three minutes the piece was over, Pamela went to commercial, and although I didn't know it at the time, that was the last I would ever hear—on that program or anywhere else.

The next day brought an hour-by-hour succession of crushing disappointments. It was a town day for Ruth, so when Karyn (my homemaker/buddy) arrived, I told her we had to be sure and watch for more details. But by the time lunch rolled around there hadn't been any mention of the researchers or their findings. Karyn left about four o'clock as she always did. Ruth got home soon after as she always did. The suppertime news rolled around as it always did. Not a word. It was almost as if it had never happened. I tried telling myself they'd make up for their silence with a hard-hitting follow-up that night, but it wasn't to be. Instead, when the evening news went to air, the nation was treated to an in-depth feature report on disreputable American dog breeders. "Killer kennels—the untold story." I couldn't believe my eyes and ears. The night before, a ninety-second story had broken that represented for thousands of dying Canadians the first real glimmer of hope this century. One short day later, the same network devoted twenty-two heart-wrenching minutes to the tragic confessions of people who had unwittingly purchased sick American puppies. Clearly, we'd lost our place in the loop, if in fact we ever had one.

Media's reaction to those researchers and their pivotal discovery convinced me more than ever that social causes ultimately rise and fall on waves that are largely outside our control. We can scream about awareness until we're blue in the face; our public fate is, in effect, the property of producers and program directors that none of us will ever see, much less influence. In order to gain favour with these architects of popular conscience, I believe we need to find ways of tying our message to one or more of three basic formats, what I refer to as the three "n"s of journalism. Beyond the standard fare of politics, sports and weather, all news can be filed under one of these "n"s: puss-n-boots, blood-n-guts or tits-n-ass. There's nothing tender or photogenic about ALS, so it's difficult to compete with things as sentimentally appealing as seal pups, endangered owls or, for that matter, flop-eared pets. And even though every couple of months, the body count matches that of some commercial airline disasters, we rarely go out with a bang. Most of us just wither away behind closed doors, so we can't compete with gory or spectacular things like car crashes, house fires or natural calamities. But the area where we seem to be lacking most is in the tits-n-ass department. Media's growing thirst for sex-related storylines is definitely where it's at in terms of future awareness prospects.

An excellent case in point—not long ago I heard one of the NBA's most celebrated basketball bumpkins telling reporters about his past sexual exploits. He admitted regularly sharing his bed with up to six women at once, contracting a sexually transmitted disease and of course, as has become the fashion, finding God. In the days that followed, I watched as he went on to achieve role-model status on every talk show and newscast from Bugtussle to Barcelona. Am I missing something, or did someone lower the standards for role models when we weren't looking? Where I come from, nobody needed a cancerous growth to realize Terry Fox was a role model. And you needn't be sitting in a wheelchair to look up to someone like Rick Hansen. Likewise, and more to the point, we don't have to test positive for a life-threatening virus to know Arthur Ashe had what it took…but Magic Johnson? I don't bear the man any personal malice, and in fact, if I could move, talk and had a small step-ladder, I'd tell him so to his face. Rather, my malice is directed at the system, a system where someone as private as Ashe could be hounded by rabid packs of reporters until forced to go public. But when someone as accessible as Johnson openly follows his million-dollar member from groupie to groupie for the better part of a career, the same jackals fall strangely silent. Then (wonder of wonders), when he catches a dose of the inevitable, it's lights, camera, action…business as usual. Rick Hansen wheels halfway around the planet before the media machine shifts out of neutral. Ervin Johnson flicks his magic bic and the same machinery slams into overdrive, presidential soap-boxes pop out, and he's served up like some kind of icon of integrity. If this doesn't smack of agenda, I don't know what does.

Another far less insidious but pretty good example is k.d. lang's recent revelation. News flash: woman in three-piece suit and barber's haircut claims to be gay. Now, k.d. happens to be one of my all-time favourites, but I can't help wondering—is this stuff really newsworthy? Didn't everyone with a pulse already have it figured out? The next thing you know, Don Cherry will be calling a press conference to announce he has poor taste in ties.

The bottom line is this: ALS, as a cause, simply isn't sexy enough. Hope springs eternal, though, and at this very moment researchers could be uncovering a common cause that's linked to something titillating. Maybe it only affects people who've done it in late-model Volkswagens. (It would serve me right for buying an import.) Who's to say exposing one's genitalia to cheap vinyl upholstery doesn't adversely affect our neuro-muscular well-being. Something like this could be all that's separating us from glittering Hollywood fundraisers and widespread media attention.

In an ideal world ALS wouldn't exist, but if someone must fall prey, nothing would further our cause quicker than if that someone were to have a high sexual profile. Somebody like Madonna would be perfect. Again, I must stress that my malice is directed at the system—not the individual—so don't misunderstand me. I wouldn't wish ALS on my worst enemy. But let's face it, if the "venereal girl's" beloved buns were to start going flat and bony before their time, you can bet your bustier the outcry would be heard around the world. It makes my nipples hard just thinking about it.

I suppose it didn't really start coming clear to me until Barbara Frum died. News of her passing brought tears to my eyes, but for the life of me, I couldn't explain why. She wasn't a close friend. I didn't even know she was seriously ill. Intuition told me she was a good and decent person, and I'll go to my grave believing her character was all it appeared to be, but with all due respect, the way the system is set up, intuition is all I have to go on. Here was a woman who'd been in my living room literally thousands of times. Over the years I'd taken her word on every topic imaginable, but couldn't say I knew the first thing about her—not a single, solitary thing. Media seems to have painted itself into an untouchable corner, a corner we aren't allowed to know.

For some unknown reason, most of us think nothing of allowing these info-gurus into our homes, night after night, no questions asked. But realistically, on what grounds are we to believe they're any more trustworthy than the people they interview? If a duly elected public official gets so much as a love letter, the juicy bits will be instantaneously spoon-fed to news hungry hordes from coast to coast to coast. Yet those who insist on smearing our screens with this kind of personal pablum face no scrutiny whatsoever. So what's the scoop on Peter Mansbridge and Wendy Mesley? Before they tied their nuptial knot was there premarital sex, and if so, how much? I want dates! I want times! I want positions! Surely, in a free and democratic society, we have a right to know these things. Who cares which politicians smoked pot? Just once I'd like to hear what some of these tele-prompted talking heads are on. Who are these people? What dark and devious reason does Jack Webster have for keeping sheep? Does Hanna Gartner sleep in her underwear, and if so, what is she trying to hide?

I don't want this to sound like I'm singling out the CBC. On the contrary, now that I receive regular newscasts from five provinces, two states and four countries, I can say with a guarded sense of pride that the Canadian Broadcasting Corporation is as good as it gets. Unfortunately, from where I sit, as good as it gets still isn't good enough. Regardless of network, the gap between documentary genius and gratuitous muckraking is narrowing. Our unbridled right to know has become their unbridled right to misinform. There seem to be some common tentacles running throughout the entire system. Bottom-feeders are rising to the surface, and there don't seem to be any safeguards to keep them from dragging standards down to their lowest common denominator. Freedom of the press, oft-touted as the cornerstone of democracy, is beginning to look more and more like a rock for industry low-lifes to hide under. The same freedom that fosters and nurtures the bravery of foreign correspondents and award-winning exposés also offers safe haven to the cut-and-dried, cut-and-paste, cut-and-run tabloids intent on polluting the airwaves. The other day we clicked on one of those daytime talk shows and Sally Jessy Raphael was playing host to a transexual, bisexual, male cross-dresser with lesbian tendencies. Given these kind of exhibitionist and exploitive broadcasting trends, and given that the programmers' penchant for one-upmanship shows no sign of abating, I have to ask, can ALSers in their wildest dreams ever hope to compete for coverage?

Speaking of wild dreams, I have a recurring fantasy. In it, a growing mob of protesters is storming Parliament Hill. On the surface they're nothing out of the ordinary…just the usual cross section of anti-everything activists and sign-waving rent-a-whiners. For argument's sake, let's call them the Friends of the People's Coalition of Raging Minorities Against Saving the Double-breasted Bureaucrat. A swelling vanguard of hastily painted picket signs bob and sway: "Honk If You Hate Bureaucrats," "Death to Bureaucrat Sympathizers," "Just Say No to Double-breasted Bureaucrats." As surveillance helicopters swoop in and hover overhead, the protesters' painfully monotonous chants grow louder: "What do we want? Everything! When do we want it? Now!" Here and there, life-size bureaucrat effigies are set ablaze as vanloads of media militia burst on the scene. With lightning speed, satellite links are established and the story goes national. Audio-visual SWAT teams spill from the vans and ready themselves for a full frontal assault. Then, waving their high-powered video bazookas and billy-club microphones, they plunge into the crowd with all the comic fervour of Keystone Kops.

Out of nowhere, a small army of crack security forces closes in forming a tight human perimeter and stands ready to disperse the unruly intruders. In a valiant show of solidarity, the protesters respond by locking arms and chanting all the louder: "Hey hey, ho ho, everything has got to go." In a futile attempt to restore order, the Executive Vice-Secretary to the Assistant Deputy Minister of Bureaucrats nervously appeals for calm (in both official languages). Then, in a brilliant manoeuvre, fifteen renegade protesters, dressed only in hospital examination gowns, break ranks, upend a pair of portable toilets and use them as battering rams to gain strategic ground on the very steps of the Legislature. Their surprise tactic throws the authorities into a momentary state of disarray, and for an instant, everything seems poised to explode. But instead of rushing the entrance, the would-be anarchists stop dead in their tracks and turn to face the crowd. An eerie hush falls over the hill. Knuckles whiten. Triggers tighten. A nation holds its breath, but the police hold their fire.

Sensing their window of opportunity, the renegades seize the moment and spring into action. In a brazen show of territorial sovereignty they pace off a symbolic line in the sand and plant their porta-potties. Then, with the disciplined grace of a seasoned drill team, they form a line, turn about-face in perfect unison and bend over. From Port Alberni to Port aux Basques, television viewers look on in stunned disbelief as fifteen flimsy gowns part and fifteen dissident backsides combine to form a desperate cry for help. From puffy sun-starved cheek to puffy sun-starved cheek, in bold black felt pen, is a lengthy string of letters:

AM YO TR OP HI C LA TE RA L SC LE RO SI S

Finally, as Canada strains to make sense of the fractured message, a pair of mock sentries emerge from the porta-potties and in a parting show of defiance, unfurl a long toilet paper banner. On it is a special message for the cameras: "ALS Coverage Really Stinks!"

My fantasy always seems to end the same chaotic way. Struggling to maintain an air of composure, stone-faced reporters scramble to sign off, but before any of them can finish, their voices are drowned out as fifteen well-placed kazoos break into a rank rendition of "Blowin' In The Wind."

I don't have any answers either. Like I said, my few direct contacts with media don't make me an expert, but I like to think I can spot a bogus bill of goods when I see one, and I can say with a certain degree of confidence that media isn't all it appears to be. Over the past few years I've run into journalists whose sensitivity and sense of professionalism is beyond reproach. Unfortunately, I've also encountered those whose sole reason for living is to stir up shit. So until reporters are obliged to submit their "stories" orally through desktop polygraph machines, it's going to be incumbent upon us all to sift through the subliminal sewage.

To the future ALSer who may choose to walk the media mine field, all I can really offer in the way of advice are a couple general pointers.

- If you expect to be misquoted, you'll tailor your comments to minimize that which can be readily misconstrued. Often one media outlet will quote the comments of another. Consequently, at least where some of my comments are concerned, I've even seen misquotes misquoted.

- If you expect to have your comments taken out of context, you'll be more likely to salt your statements with what I call "focus phrases"—something that encapsulates the gist of your message in a few carefully chosen words. That way, when they arbitrarily decide to pluck something, you, the pluckee, stand a better chance of being properly plucked. If you're unprepared or unable to package your thoughts into the allotted number of seconds or column inches, someone will do it for you…it's their job.

- Above all, as ethically challenged as some of these people may seem at first, try to remember that they're just people. Beyond the inaccuracies, supposition, conjecture, personal bias and innuendo, they're really just one group of human beings telling another group of human beings that which they deem worth telling. For every unscrupulous reporter, there's one who'll do you justice, and if you're patient, the good ones will eventually find you.

Sometimes, in my zeal to be heard, I feel like an annoying little mongrel yapping at the heels of a big, unpredictable bull. One well-placed kick could knock me right out of the barn, but sooner or later, one of us is going to have to move. This is my way of saying that I know what I'm doing. I realize using a book to sort out my feelings is tantamount to placing my neck on a chopping block. If the axe falls, so be it. I don't have time to beat around the bush.

For me, media has been a world of princes and thieves…a world where rival electronic empires compete for the same basic truths. Within these empires, I suspect opposing forces wage noble internal wars over what to leave in and what to leave out, but noble as these wars may be, they are ultimately determined not so much by principle as by deadlines, double standards and the almighty rating point. Only when competition thrives can sensationalism thrive. And only when sensationalism thrives can unsensational causes like ALS go virtually unreported.

To this point, I've tried to articulate
how past events have shaped
the way I feel about dying,
but I haven't done a great job
explaining what those
feelings really are.
Typical or unique,
right or wrong,
I'm an expert in the field.

18

To Die or Not to Die

Remember Nancy B.? She's the young Ontario woman who, after a lengthy court case, won the right to die. The right to die? It has an oppressive ring to it, don't you think? Kind of like the right to take a dump. Five billion people are walking this earth (give or take a few hundred million), and it's reasonable to assume that every last one of them is going to die. There's no getting around it—death is a fact of life. That said, it seems truly preposterous that some of us have to fight for the right to do it on our own terms. So when the folks at "Morningside" asked if I could make some comment, I considered their request for about a millisecond and gestured to Ruth for my computer.

CBC "Morningside"

Dear Peter,

By the time you read this, Nancy B. may well have made her final decision. For what it's worth, the disease that's killing me also leads to artificial life support, so Nancy's story is very near to my heart. The colossal arrogance of those who've chosen to chastise Nancy incites in me both anger and fear. The notion that other people want to dictate mine or anyone else's longevity scares me far more than death itself. What is more sinister, allowing someone to die, or forcing someone to live?

I'm not sure if we're losing sight of reality, or if technology is blinding us to it. We've reached a point where life can legally begin in a test tube, legally end in the hands of professional abortionists, and be legally, artificially and forcibly prolonged against our will. Over time, allowing nature to take its course seems to have become a non-option, so in my mind, the single most important word in the judge's ruling was "nature." By putting his ruling in these terms, he has appealed to a higher law. Nevertheless, though I'm not a religious man, it's hard to deny the legitimacy of white-coated gods with the power to turn life on and off at will.

Today we have machines that can breathe for us. Maybe tomorrow they'll invent a machine that keeps us conscious by slapping our face at regular intervals. I can already hear the morality squad urging me on. "Come on Dennis, just one more slap for mankind, a cure is just around the corner."

By definition I may be helpless, but if I am forced to stare at the ceiling of an intensive-care unit for one second beyond that which I deem my natural life, then, and only then, will I truly feel helpless.

I am heading into my seventh year fighting a disease I was told would take me in three, so believe me when I say that I don't advocate throwing in the towel. I merely respect Nancy's need to control her own life. Perhaps a day is coming when my wife, who caters to my every whim, will falter and I, like Nancy B., will want to decide my own fate. I have outlined my wishes in a living will, but the ongoing debate makes me wonder if it will be worth the paper it's written on.

To die, or not to die…that is not the question at all. The real question is, do we have the right to live the lives we choose? Life was meant to be lived, not frantically clutched like some last crust of bread.

Sincerely,

The Incredible Shrinking Man

Footnote: *On January 6, 1992, Quebec Superior Court Justice Jacques Dufour granted Nancy's request. A thirty-day mandatory appeal period was imposed and respected. Seven days later, on the thirteenth of February, respiratory life-support was discontinued and she was allowed to die. Nancy was 25.*

When I started this book, I never intended to make any blanket statements on euthanasia, so in a way, what follows is another classic example of how a disease like ALS can turn a person's sensibilities inside out. At the time I felt neither qualified nor comfortable passing judgment on so personal an issue, and it still makes me feel uncomfortable, but in light of growing controversy, my silence has become a personal liability. If I am to counter those who would control me, then this chapter becomes strategically imperative. My hope is this: the more people who know my wishes, the less likely any one person will be to defy them.

As my physical free fall drags on, it's getting harder and harder to envision actually hitting bottom. Put another way, you can only die for so long before you have to call it living.

But even so, I harbour no illusions. Death will come, and when it does, the muscles controlling my lungs show every sign of being the last things to go. This makes me a prime candidate for a procedure I object to with every fibre of my bony being. It's called a tracheostomy.

It's a sorry scenario indeed that someone in my position would so mistrust the system that he feels he must make his most private wishes a matter of public record. Please understand that my motives are purely selfish and should in no way be construed as an attempt to sway the morals of others. If you like, you can think of the following waiver as a literary pre-emptive strike.

> In the event of respiratory failure, I, Dennis Kaye,
> being of sound mind, do hereby declare invasive surgery
> for the purpose of permanent life support
> to be a violation of my person.
> Any physician, emergency field personnel or other health-
> care worker who performs, authorizes to perform, or assists
> in performing the aforementioned assault will
> be subject to litigation.

Whether you agree or not is neither here nor there, but because this subject evokes such strong emotions, I feel a sense of obligation to explain my reasoning fully.

Because ALS affects different people in dramatically different ways, its victims face a variety of different choices. There are those who can neither breathe nor eat without mechanical aids, but are still able to speak and walk. On the other end of the spectrum are people like myself. With difficulty, I'm still able to breathe and swallow, but my speech is almost unintelligible, and I haven't moved anything but my head without help for years.

It could be that I—like many invalids—have become more perceptive than the average individual, including those individuals in the medical profession. Or maybe there's just less of me to figure out (ninety pounds and dropping). Whatever the reason, I believe these past few years have put me in tune with my body in ways even the most qualified physician couldn't possibly understand. Still, in some ways I think the medical monster is one of our own creation. Doctors are expected to decide so much so often, it only follows that they would eventually develop a false sense of omnipotence. This isn't an excuse, it's an observation. The decision to sustain or suspend life is not a responsibility they demand, it's one they accept, and in my view, it simply isn't fair to repeatedly burden any human being with the ultimate fate of another.

This is what, in Nancy B.'s case, made Justice Dufour's actions so courageous. Leaving robes, lawyers, court recorders and a parade of expert witnesses behind, he chose to meet one on one with Nancy. In this vulnerable new atmosphere, the good judge's lofty Latin decrees would have meant nothing. All that would have mattered would have been the message, the moment and the look in Nancy's eyes.

It's been called everything from mercy to murder—final exit, self-deliverance, the ultimate painkiller, death with dignity, biting the big banana. Call it what you want, I believe the whole debate over euthanasia has been fundamentally flawed from the start. In fact, if you accept dictionary definitions, there's no such thing as "passive euthanasia." Euthanasia is pro-active by definition, and unless I have Alzheimer's too, being passively pro-active is an impossibility. Like planned spontaneity, it's clearly a contradiction in terms. Passive euthanasia simply allows death to occur, while active euthanasia clearly causes it, so defining both with the same word is just asking for trouble. Until we acknowledge them as totally separate issues, finding a common consensus on either one will remain an impossibility.

Another important factor that seems to get lost in the shuffle is the way we exclude the acts of caregivers from our normal definition of "life support." The average healthy individual thinks only in terms of tubes, wires and high technology, but each time my wife spoon-feeds me I'm reminded that in the truest sense of the words I too am on life support. It's imperative people understand that sometimes refusing treatment means much more than simply pulling a plug, flipping a switch or withholding a utility payment. For some, the one and only option is starvation.

Other variables also cloud the issue. Is there uncontrollable pain? Is there consciousness? Has brain death been established? Is the person physically able to perform the act alone, or will it require a second party? What waivers, if any, affect the life insurance? Is religion involved? Some folks are content to live by the dictates of Church or State; others are not. And perhaps the most important question of all: Is there hope? At the end of the day, can anyone guarantee life is worth living without it, and if so, on whose authority?

Solving the impasse and answering the litany of questions that surround it is going to take a great deal of compromise. Until that compromise is reached, I'm afraid that supporting or opposing euthanasia in any form or in any situation will mean offending someone.

Not long ago, my doctor dropped in for a visit, and as he moved his stethoscope around my chest, I whimsically asked if I was still alive. He assured me I was, but then his voice took on an uncharacteristically serious tone. He described my breathing as "superficial." At the time, I wasn't sure what he meant by superficial, but the way he said it told me the time had come to make my feelings known in no uncertain terms. On that score alone, I hope this chapter has helped. We all hope for the best, but I believe 125 years of near-fruitless research gives me the right to prepare for the worst.

Who knows? Maybe when the time comes I'll chicken out. I guess all I really want is the security of knowing I still have a hand in my destiny.

In thought lies power.
Words are just a medium;
speech…a mere conduit.
Expecting or allowing others
to channel our power can strain
the best of friendships and lead
the most noble intention astray.

19

The Whole Truth and Nothing But the Truth

I n August of 1991 a young Victoria, B.C., woman named Sue Rodriguez was diagnosed with ALS. For her, the disease struck with a vengeance. By the time eight months had passed she'd lost the dexterity in both hands and the strength in both legs, and she had already taken several nasty falls. For Sue there was never any question. She wants to die at a time of her choosing, but realized early on that it would almost certainly require the assistance of a second party. In Canada, suicide is not a criminal offence, but assisting someone, regardless of their disability, is. In April of 1992 Sue purchased a copy of *Final Exit,* the suicide manual by Derek Humphry. It answered the practical questions, but not the legal ones.

In August, one year after her diagnosis, she sought the help of the Right to Die Society of Canada and, in particular, a man named John Hofsess. A contract was forged and together they started a legal ball rolling from the Supreme Court of British Columbia, through the B.C. Court of Appeal and ultimately to the Supreme Court of Canada.

Her petition was extremely personal in nature, but equally far-reaching in its implications: for herself and for others, she was petitioning for the right to assistance in ending her own life. If successful, Sue Rodriguez would shake the very foundations of a law that has stood since 1892. Naturally, this court challenge brought widespread media attention and I, like millions of others, was introduced to Sue through the lens of a television camera. The weakness in her voice touched me deeply. The strength in her words touched me more.

December 31, 1992

CBC "Morningside"

Dear Peter,

Well, I couldn't stand it any longer. I had to put my two cents in on the Sue Rodriguez case. Not since Nancy B. has a story struck closer to home. It's as if the issue were a stone dropped in a pond, with rings of rhetoric spreading in every direction. Everybody and their dog is talking about it: government officials, theologians, doctors, lawyers, Geraldo. Strangely enough, none of these people are actually dying. They talk and talk, but in all likelihood, won't face what they're talking about for another thirty or forty years. I hear "experts" say things like, "We deal with death every day," when in reality they will deal with death but once. I don't care if they have masters degrees in forensic pathology, their opinions are inherently invalid.

To make matters worse, be they religious, medical or judiciary potentates, they answer to powerful administrative bodies and elite fraternities…rarely to the individuals they wish to control. Whether by accident or by design, I'm convinced it's this airtight bubble of endless appeals and bureaucratic buck-passing that insures no one ever need shoulder direct responsibility. And while the same tired old machinery grinds on, Sue draws ever and ever closer to the very end she so desperately wants to avoid.

We have a saying in the ALS community: "Where there's hope there's life." Well unfortunately, for some, hope will never spring eternal, nor is it something that can be prescribed or legislated. I have a theory. If the moral minority were to redirect even a fraction of the energy they expend finding fault into finding cures, many of our worst diseases would go the way of the Bubonic Plague.

Unlike all the so-called experts and self-appointed spokespeople, I'm reluctant to comment on anyone's behalf but my own. As usual, my primary concern is ALS awareness, and I still believe it to be the key to our ever acquiring adequate research funding. Whether or not I agree with Sue's legal pursuits has become irrelevant. I've been losing ground against this disease for seven years, and in a few short months Sue has brought ALS into more homes across this ill-informed nation than all the advocacy groups, society boards and public awareness committees put together. Watching her struggle through the jungle of cameras and microphones, I can only look on with awe at her courage and determination.

In the final analysis, one day, a cure is going to be found, and when it is, hopefully some of the "morally correct" will remember an important part of that cure belongs to Sue Rodriguez. I, for one, will be grateful as long as I live.

Yours as always,
The Incredible Shrinking Man

Shortly after this letter aired, a disturbing chain of events unfolded which knocked me right off stride. It all started with an affidavit filed in B.C.'s Court of Appeal by the executive director of British Columbia's ALS Society. Composed at the request of the pro-life lobby, this document was in direct opposition to Sue, and it touched off a paper feud between the Right to Die, Right to Life and ALS Societies, not to mention newspapers from one end of the country to the other. The opinions expressed by this individual were not and are not (repeat) *were not* and *are not* sanctioned by the Amyotrophic Lateral Sclerosis Society. Nevertheless, they left a false impression with the western press in particular, and subsequently with their subscribers, that Society members were uniformly opposed to the efforts of Sue Rodriguez.

Up to that point I had considered myself to be on the sidelines of Sue's struggle, and I still see things that way, (in truth we've never met). But for reasons I still don't fully understand I began taking the words of her detractors very personally. At that time, all contact with Sue had to be made through the Right to Die Society, and with their help, I made a point of collecting every pertinent letter I could get Ruth's hands on.

This flurry of correspondence would have remained neatly tucked away in our fax file had it not been for a neighbour and good friend of ours named David Broadland. Dave lives in the next bay and paddles over from time to time to cheer Ruth up, listen to me mumble and pig out on our goodies. Dave is, himself, a small-p publisher, and as luck would have it, some of these letters were still lying around our living room during one of his visits. After he got the gist of their content he pointed out that, whether I realized it or not, I had become party to something of fundamental importance. He felt a behind-the-scenes exchange was exactly what was missing from the debate and convinced me to include it in my book. Since then, I've second-guessed David's advice a dozen times (mostly because I'm not very proud of some of my comments), but in the end I decided he was right.

As you might expect, inflammatory parts of the controversy were carried on front pages throughout the province, and as you might also expect, retractions and rebuttals were discreetly, effectively and repeatedly buried or ignored. So if nothing else, an unfiltered account like the following might help some people better appreciate that things are seldom as simple as we think, and never as simple as headlines suggest.

Regardless of their source, letters have a way of speaking for themselves, so I've resisted the temptation to editorialize, with the exception of some brief explanatory comments. All letters appear uncut and in the order they were sent and received. In hindsight, some will seem prophetic, but most stand out as unpleasant reminders of how, in matters of life and death, polarization serves no one.

Note: I am a member of the ALS Society. While I may agree with some aspects of both the Right to Die and Right to Life Societies, I choose to affiliate myself with neither.

First contact...

November 25, 1992

Dear Sue,

My name is Dennis Kaye, I'm almost at the eight-year mark with ALS, and I've been following your story. For what it's worth, I admire your courage, and agree wholeheartedly with what you're trying to accomplish.

This issue you're taking on is so universally compelling, the media will no doubt pursue your efforts to the very end. It's for this reason that I respectfully offer this reminder for future interviews. In BCTV's recent feature on your video address to the Standing Committee, you said you had no desire to wait until you were "reduced to a mere biological existence." I know it wasn't your intention, but coming from someone in much better shape than me, it was a painful thing to hear. Physically, I'm completely helpless, and even though I have to type with a stupid-looking contraption on my head, on good days, I like to think I'm more than that.

Anyway, I and a few million other people are truly grateful for what you're doing. If you think of some way I can help, please feel free to call or fax.

Go get 'em Sue.

Sincerely yours,

Dennis

December 12, 1992

Mr. Dennis Kaye

Dear Dennis,

I read your letter of November 25 with very mixed feelings.

On the one hand, I was very touched by your wholehearted support of what I'm trying to do. I've heard a lot about you and I admire the work that you do. That you would so strongly offer your support and encouragement means more to me than I can adequately convey in words.

On the other hand, I was very dismayed to realize that my poor choice of words had caused you (and no doubt others) pain. At the time of the video taping, which was a rather stressful experience, I'm afraid I wasn't thinking about the impact my words might have on other ALS sufferers; I was focused on trying to get my message across to members of the Standing Committee, as effectively as possible. I now deeply regret this short-sightedness.

I am still getting used to the idea that, like it or not, I have become a very public figure and that this means I have a responsibility to, at minimum, avoid offending or hurting those individuals for whom I may have become a spokesperson.

Thank you for the insights you have given me, and keep up the good work!

Sincerely,

Sue Rodriguez

P.S. This letter has been prepared in accordance with my verbal instructions, by a neighbour who has kindly offered her assistance with my correspondence.

The affidavit...

IN THE SUPREME COURT OF BRITISH COLUMBIA

BETWEEN:

SUE RODRIQUEZ [*sic*]

PETITIONER

AND:

ATTORNEY GENERAL OF BRITISH COLUMBIA
ATTORNEY GENERAL OF CANADA
AFFIDAVIT

I, RHELDA EVANS, of 411 Dunsmuir St., Vancouver British Columbia, SWEAR AS FOLLOWS:

1. I am the Executive Director of the ALS Society and have been so for 2 years and I have worked for the ALS Society for 4 1/2 years.
2. The ALS Society has about 550 members and was founded by Roy Slater in 1981 to help sufferers of Lou Gehrig's Disease.
3. Apart from administration, I counsel those who suffer from the disease providing information about medical, financial, nursing, hospital, equipment, spiritual and emotional support for them and for their families.

4. Usually the disease is not painful but patients do suffer the problems set out in the Petitioner's Affidavit.
5. Equipment and treatment is available to relieve all of the physical symptoms and disabilities to a certain extent. In particular wheelchairs, ventilators, feeding tubes, voice synthesizers and other devices and also healthcare workers, nurses, psychiatrists, psychologists, Doctors and other professionals and also palliative care and hospice units.
6. Fear and the emotional and spiritual problems are also relieved effectively by appropriate counselling, psychiatric and psychological treatment, but most particularly by love and care and sympathy.
7. Each year there are about 55 deaths amongst our members, but only about one attempted suicide a year and to my knowledge there have been no suicides amongst our members. Those who have attempted suicide have obtained greater attention from their families, professionals and care givers and have been treated successfully for their depression.
8. I have only had experience with one woman who needed to be sedated whilst dying because of fear and in fact most patients die in their sleep.
9. Some patients who were prolonging their lives with treatment by life support systems have asked to have them turned off, but that is not suicide.
10. It is most important to emphasize to a patient that it is better to spend your energy and time on making the best of living rather than on deciding whether to die.
11. It is important for the patient to avoid fixating on the disasters which may happen instead of looking at the possibilities of making the best of what they have.
12. I have spoken to a very large number of our members with ALS; none of them want the law changed since they are satisfied with the options available to them: their right to refuse treatment for the prolongation of life and their right to sedation.

Sworn before me at Vancouver, in
the Province of British Columbia
this 11 day of December 1992.

Rhelda Evans

I'm not impressed...

RE: Sue Rodriguez & Damage Control

Dear Rhelda,

As an individual you are free, as are we all, to express yourself
wherever and however you choose, but your behaviour as Executive
Director is an entirely different matter. Regarding your now famous
Supreme Court Affidavit, by using 411 Dunsmuir as your address and
your directorship as a soap box you have, in my opinion, over-stepped
your authority by a country mile. I may be ignorant when it comes to
Society protocol, but as an ALSer, I don't believe members of the
executive (past presidents and doctors included) have either the
mandate or the qualifications to speak on my behalf in matters as
personal as suicide.

Your assertion (item 12) that ALSers are of one mind on the
Rodriguez issue is at best inaccurate, and at worst, blatantly misleading. Considering the Victoria Chapter is roughly split down the
middle, either some clients have been deliberately avoiding the
Vancouver office, or you were overly selective about who you chose
to poll. Perhaps Jenny Young's legitimate and timely survey will support my contention that opinion among the terminally ill is, in fact,
anything but unanimous. Many of us may disagree with Sue's rationale, but this doesn't mean many of us don't also wish her well in
her legal bid for peace of mind. I was truly stunned by your second-
hand reference to her, on CBC Radio, as "that awful woman." I have
corresponded with Sue directly, and respectfully submit that she is

neither awful, nor, as your affidavit suggests, a victim of depression. If, however, constant opposition leads to depression or, heaven forbid, accelerates her plans even by an hour, must I as a Society member be forced to share in the blame?

I also have a purely selfish reason for voicing my disapproval. In physical, emotional and financial terms, I have invested very heavily in my most recent awareness campaign. By unilaterally aligning us with a group as politically volatile as the Pro-Life lobby, you may have already undermined my efforts in a very big way. Even though we're clearly not dealing with a defenceless fetus, if the Society's reputation becomes one of being openly partisan or secular, we run a very real risk of alienating a huge block of potential support.

I've come to learn that, despite my requests to do so, invitations to join my campaign were withheld from the board. I trust this fax won't meet the same fate. Please present it as my contribution to Tuesday's meeting.

Make no mistake, I admire your administrative abilities, and have no doubt you are following your heart, but in the interests of the entire membership, it's imperative the board reach a consensus and make it public immediately. If, by some stretch of the imagination, they take a position other than complete neutrality, I can only wonder at the Society's future.

Sincerely,

Dennis Kaye

Note: At the time this letter was written, Jenny Young, a Vancouver-based social worker and Society board member, was conducting an in-depth survey of thirteen ALS patients ranging in age from thirty-six to seventy. All were on or soon to be on mechanical ventilation. Every patient interviewed stated that they, alone, should make the final decision concerning life support. But roughly half showed no desire to be mechanically supported, and factors considered when making their decisions were as varied as the survey's participants.

The Right to Die Society wades in…

The Right to Die Society of Canada
P.O. Box 39018, Victoria, B.C. V8V 4X8

Tuesday, January 19, 1993

FAX transmission
ALS Society of British Columbia
411 Dunsmuir, 2nd Flr,
Vancouver, B.C. V6B 1X4
Attention: Allan Graham, President

Dear Mr. Graham,

I am writing on behalf of Sue Rodriguez:

She read in the *Vancouver Sun* that the ALS Society of B.C. passed a resolution last Tuesday vowing itself to be "neutral" on the issue of her current court action in which she seeks a physician's eventual assistance in dying.

She has not received word of the formal text of the resolution and therefore may not understand its intent perfectly. However she wishes to point out that on December 17, 1992, the ProLife Society of B.C., which is one of two intervenors in the case actively opposed to Sue Rodriguez's petition, submitted affidavits by Roy Slater and Rhelda Evans in support of the ProLife's Society's position.

The sworn affidavit by Rhelda Evans included such sentences as: "*I Rhelda Evans of 411 Dunsmuir Street…am the Executive Director of the ALS Society and have been so for 2 years… Apart from administration, I counsel those who suffer from the disease providing information about medical, financial, nursing, hospital,*

The Whole Truth and Nothing But the Truth 213

equipment, spiritual and emotional support for them and their families.... I have spoken to a very large number of our members with ALS; none of them want the law changed since they are satisfied with the options available to them..." and so on.

These affidavits by Roy Slater and Rhelda Evans continue to exert an effect upon the courts as they are part of the documents that will now go to the B.C. Court of Appeal of February 15th, and beyond that to the Supreme Court of Canada; moreover, nothing prevents the lawyer, Mr. Ace Henderson, who represents the ProLife Society of B.C., from continuing to refer to these documents in his arguments. Whenever Mr. Henderson refers to either of these documents he stresses the direct link they have to the ALS Society and depicts Sue Rodriguez thereby as an eccentric individual and by no means typical judged by ALS Society standards as enunciated by Rhelda Evans and Roy Slater.

It is Sue Rodriguez's contention that if the ALS Society of B.C. is truly "neutral" in any meaningful sense of the word, it will require that these affidavits be withdrawn from further use by lawyer Mr. Henderson and further influence upon the courts.

Sue Rodriguez looks forward to your reply as soon as possible. She already suffers enough from people trying to impose their values upon her without the ALS Society—directly or indirectly—opposing her in the courts while proclaiming its "neutrality" in the media.

Yours respectfully,
John Hofsess
Executive Director.

Note: Though Roy Slater's name appears in a negative context, his affidavit reflected his personal position and did not implicate others in any way. Roy died on August 14, 1993. He was my friend.

Dear John,

One request, a couple questions and one offer.

Requests—

We're pretty much out of touch up here on Quadra Island. I'd really appreciate it if you could fax a copy of the newspaper article where Allan Graham's comments appear.

Questions—

1) Is Sue registered as a member with the ALS Society and if so, does she receive their notices, newsletters, etc.?

2) Through all this affidavit fiasco, has anyone on the Vancouver Board had the balls to correspond directly with Sue, or does she rely entirely on the media for knowledge of what they're up to?

Offer—

Personally, although I disagree, I don't have a big problems with Roy's affidavit. It's Rhelda's comments and the way she misrepresented the Society that got my hackles up. If you're unsuccessful in getting a retraction, I'd like Sue to know that if she needs a "personal" affidavit, she can count on me. I'm no lawyer, but might it not be even more advantageous to discredit the contents of the previous affidavits than to merely have them discounted?

As for your letter to Allan, I agree with every word.

Sincerely yours,

Dennis Kaye

A.L.S. Society of British Columbia

January 21, 1993

Mr. John Hofsess
P.O. Box 39018
Victoria, B.C.
V8V 4X8

Dear Mr. Hofsess:
Re: Affidavits

Neither affiant was authorized by the Society to make the affidavit and neither affidavit contained any reference to the affiant being so authorized.

Allan Graham, President

Sue Rodriguez c/o John Hofsess

Dear Sue,

I share your frustration, I share your anger, and if it's possible, I believe I share your pain. In my view, Allan Graham's behaviour is clearly inflammatory and even though it's not reflective of the membership, I fully understand your need to use his ignorance to your advantage even if it may jeopardize the Society's public profile.

I only have one selfish request for you to consider before making this matter public. I've just spent the last year of my life raising private money and private support to produce and broadcast the public service announcement that's presently airing throughout B.C. (maybe you've seen it). Needless to say, I'm extremely worried that if the entire Society is painted with the same brush, all my efforts may well go right down the tube. I've been unable, in the past five years, to convince the board of the validity of this kind of campaign, and sincerely believe they're finally starting to see the light.

As you'll see from the following copies, I've done my best to defend your position from within. All I ask in return is that you temper your public statements in such a way as to make one thing clear…it is a very select few who are hiding behind the Society to further their own agendas. The Society does so much wonderful work, I can only hope the general public won't turn its back on the whole organization.

I wish you strength and a fond good-luck in the coming appeal. I'll be there in spirit.

Sincerely yours,
Dennis Kaye

A request for help…

Tuesday, January 26, 1993

Attention: Dennis Kaye

Sue's lawyer, Chris Considine, says that he would welcome an affidavit from you if that can be arranged before February 10th.

There has been no further reply from Allan Graham. It appears as if he is determined to "stonewall" on the issue of withdrawing Rhelda's statements. Does one just accept that?

Do you have any other suggestions for individuals who might be willing to contribute an affidavit upholding Sue's right to make a choice?

Thanks for your time and concern.

John Hofsess

The papermill grinds on…

January 27, 1993

ALS Society of B.C.
Attention: Mr. Allan Graham—ALS Society President
From: Dennis Kaye

Dear Allan:

My letter of January 23/93 was not an attempt to ascertain your legal opinion. I was writing to Allan Graham (the Society President) not Allan Graham (the lawyer).

The point is not whether the affidavits were or were not authorized.
The point is not whether you, I, Sue or anyone else agrees with their contents.
And *the point* is not whether it can or cannot be successfully argued that the affidavits influence our neutrality.
The point is that it *will* be argued, and that the argument *will* itself be harmful to the Society!

It would appear from your seeming unwillingness to address the point, coupled with John Hofsess' latest fax, and the comments of Sue Rodriguez therein, that my earlier prediction is already on the verge of coming true.

When the shit hits the fan, whether we like it or not, most of it is going to land squarely at 411 Dunsmuir Street.

Sincerely,
Dennis Kaye

Right to Die Society
Attention: John Hofsess

Dear John:

Don't ask me why, but Campbell River's Commissioner for Taking Affidavits is limited to only certain kinds of affidavits, and the one I would do is not one of them. However, we did find a lawyer whose office is accessible, but the procedure could run as high as one hundred dollars. It that's ok, we'll fill out as much as possible in advance and go to Campbell River early next week. I imagine we'll need case numbers and such like. Keep me posted.

Sincerely yours,

Dennis Kaye

John steps over the line...

The Right to Die Society of Canada
P.O. Box 39018, Victoria, B.C. V8V 4X8

Thursday, January 28, 1993

Attn: VOICES
Shelley Fralic
Deputy Managing Editor
From: John Hofsess

On January 14th, I submitted a short "letter to the editor" conveying the message—at Sue Rodriguez's request—that the press release issued by the ALS Society of B.C. that it was officially "neutral" in regard to the issue of assisted suicide, was less than honest for various reasons. Unfortunately either the letter was never received or, unaccountably, the basic point made in the letter was not considered noteworthy. In any event it has not been published.

Sue Rodriguez considers the issue to be extremely important to her and to others in B.C. with ALS who must deal with this Society—which claims to represent their interests but has little respect for them as individuals.

She has therefore drafted this commentary for your VOICES column and hopes very much it will be found worthy of publication. Please advise.

John Hofsess

Note: Without Sue's knowledge, but in what is perceived to be her best interests, John Hofsess composes and puts Sue's initials to a letter which he then submits to the *Vancouver Sun.* It goes as follows:

VOICES section
Vancouver Sun

Of Human Bondage
by Sue Rodriguez

These are the final months of my life.

With each passing week there are new diminishments of my former self. Four weeks ago I was forced to realize I could no longer feed myself. My hands don't obey my brain anymore. My voice is often so weak nowadays that I can barely speak. None of these aggravations incline me to look forward to my death. The fact is, I love life and always have.

But I can see myself being whittled away like a piece of wood; little by little there is less and less. And I know the day is approaching faster than I would like when I will say: enough is enough. I am not Sue Rodriguez any longer. This is not—for me—an acceptable quality of life.

Unlike some individuals with ALS I have never enjoyed what is called a "plateau"—a period of relative stability. I have had no opportunity to develop a new vision of myself as a capable albeit disabled person. Last summer I could walk and run. Today I can barely stand. ALS is attacking me rapidly and relentlessly.

Yet lately I have come to realize that my illness is not the worst part of the ordeal I face. More and more I have to contend with human perversity. I do not mean simply the resistance of the provincial and federal governments to my petition for physician-assisted suicide. Nor the efforts of "prolife" groups to impose their will wherever they can. I refer to the organization which is supposed to help people like myself—the ALS Society of B.C.—which has done nothing but compound my misery.

On December 17th, two "prolife" groups sought to be granted intervenor status by the B.C. Supreme Court. This meant that in addition to challenging the Attorney General of B.C. and the Attorney General of Canada for the right to make a personal decision concerning my own body and life, I also had to contend with third-party arguments by groups opposed to my beliefs and values.

The law prohibiting assisted suicide has not been evoked once in Canada in the last 30 years. Yet now that I was asking, as a terminally ill person, to have this law interpreted in such a way as to grant me a small measure of mercy, suddenly it was a law that had to be vigorously defended by the Attorneys General as if the future of civilization depended upon it. I, who had no funds and little strength, found myself pitted against groups and institutions with virtually unlimited funds and tireless dedication to silencing my voice and crushing me.

Even worse—two officials of the ALS Society of B.C., executive director Rhelda Evans and past-president Roy Slater—filed affidavits for use by the ProLife Society of B.C., publicly criticizing me and opposing my petition. Mr. Slater depicted me as a loser, "a quitter" unlike himself who with the help of God and family had coped well with ALS for over ten years. The well-known fact that ALS affects different people differently is nowhere recognized in Mr. Slater's ideological attack. Rhelda Evans went further: "I have spoken to a very large number of our members with ALS; none of them want the law changed." I was depicted as an eccentric and depressed individual making a weird request of the courts.

When word of these affidavits got out, controversy was provoked among people with ALS. To such a degree that on January 12th, the Board of Directors of the ALS Society of B.C. held a meeting and passed a resolution that its *official* position was one that neither condemned nor condoned assisted suicide. When this was reported in the *Vancouver Sun* (Jan. 13) I felt certain that the two prejudicial affidavits would be withdrawn from future court use—at the B.C. Court of Appeal (Feb. 15) and the Supreme Court of Canada.

But when I inquired of President Allan Graham if this was indeed the case, I received the following one-line response: "Neither affiant was authorized by the Society to make the affidavit and neither affidavit contained any reference to the affiant being so authorized."

That's it. Curt, cold and heartless. I asked for honesty—I got hypocrisy. In court these misleading affidavits will continue to be used as representing the views of the ALS Society of B.C. Judges will continue to see me (falsely) condemned by my peers.

ALS is a terrible disease but the greatest handicap of all is finding oneself at the mercy of an organization which imposes a religiously-oriented mindset upon the people it claims to help and which treats people like me with open contempt.

I hope that if there is anyone who has the misfortune to be familiar with ALS who reads these words that they will write to me c/o The Right to Die Society of Canada, P.O. Box 39018, Victoria, B.C., V8V 4X8. Perhaps if enough of us speak out, the ALS Society of B.C. will yet be induced to "do the right thing." Is it too much to ask that this world afford me a small display of human decency before I die?

SR

Things get messy…

***Vancouver Sun,* Monday, Feb. 1, 1993**

Assisted Suicide
Right to Die Society shaken by forgery

Kevin Griffin—*Vancouver Sun*

A shaken John Hofsess of the Right to Die Society plans to talk with Sue Rodriguez today about his decision to forge her signature on a letter sent to *The Vancouver Sun*.

Hofsess said from Victoria the controversy over the letter and signature has depressed him by adding to the stress around Rodriguez's controversial legal fight to change the assisted suicide law.

"It is an unfortunate incident and I want to meet with Sue to reflect and learn about it and make sure it does not happen again," Hofsess said Sunday from Victoria.

Rodriguez said Friday statements critical of the ALS Society of B.C., which were attributed to her by *The Vancouver Sun,* were not her words. The statements were part of a personal letter ostensibly composed and signed by her; in fact, Hofsess has admitted he composed the letter and faked her signature.

"I did not make those comments nor would I, and I am sorry they were said," Rodriguez said.

In the past, Rodriguez has given her consent to letting the Right to Die Society speak on her behalf. As well, Hofsess said he has previously prepared statements for Rodriguez that the 42-year-old Saanich woman has approved without changes, or with very minor ones.

Hofsess said in this case, he was reluctant to call Rodriguez because of a number of health problems she has developed recently.

Asked whether the incident would mar Right to Die's credibility, Hofsess said: "I have no idea."

"I think it would be very unfortunate if it does," he said. "Obviously Sue has reached the point where people have to speak for her."

Rodriguez suffers from amyotrophic lateral sclerosis, often called Lou Gehrig's disease after the baseball legend who died of it in 1941.

ALS is a progressive and incurable degenerative nerve disease that usually kills within three years of diagnosis. But about 20 percent of those diagnosed with ALS live up to 10 years or longer.

"You have to put it in its broadest context that Sue at this point has reached a point in her disease where she cannot feed herself," Hofsess said. "It should be no surprise to anyone that she does not write her own letters."

Hofsess said he believed he was accurately reflecting Rodriguez's views on a specific issue—the politics of the ALS Society—and was acting as if he were her proxy.

Hofsess said he doesn't believe the incident will be perceived by the public as an indication he has manipulated Rodriguez.

"I don't think a letter concerning the politics of the ALS Society of B.C. indicates that I am manipulating Sue," he said. "We personally have nothing to gain by that."

Rodriguez said earlier in *The Vancouver Sun* the incident has not in any way affected her desire to change the assisted-suicide law.

Her ongoing legal battle is scheduled to be heard in the B.C. Court of Appeal on Monday, Feb. 15.

Suicide is legal in Canada. But it is illegal to counsel or assist someone to kill themselves. Rodriguez wants the right to a physician's help should she decide to take her own life as her health declines.

February 1, 1993

Right to Die Society
Attention: Mr. John Hofsess

Dear John:

I have my lawyer's appointment set for the 4th, and the better part of my statement is organized, but in light of today's *Vancouver Sun* article, I have to admit I'm a little disillusioned. In your defence, I've had my words twisted so often by media that as awful as the articles sound, I take for granted the article's accuracy probably lands somewhere between gospel truth and bold-faced lies.

I still want to help, but under the circumstances I'm sure you'll understand that if I am to proceed with any measure of confidence, I'll need to speak once with Sue directly (please provide her number ASAP). When Sue assures me first-hand that I should continue corresponding through your Society, I'll feel a lot better.

Just what we needed, eh?

Sincerely yours,
Dennis Kaye

Tuesday, February 2, 1993

Dear Dennis,

I agree that you should touch base with Sue before proceeding with your affidavit. To the best of my knowledge, she welcomes your affidavit and so does our lawyer Chris Considine. I am meeting with Sue on Wednesday for an extended talk in which we must review a wide range of issues in order to ensure that I, once again, feel confident that I understand her wishes. My sense is—that as her energy flags—she is less and less willing to become embroiled in political disputes even when her interests are at stake. She calls it "bashing"— doctors, home care workers, etc.—even when she has completely legitimate complaints. And so my opinion piece (a Voices column, not a letter) which I initialized (not "forged her signature"), which I submitted because *The Sun* had refused to publish my own letter (succinct and certainly worthy of publication) covering the same points—unexpectedly ran counter to Sue's current mood of tolerating everyone's behaviour and opinion without critical comment.

Best time to reach Sue is mid to late morning when her homecare worker Nadine is there. Sue's private unlisted number is ——; it may however be best to try the regular line first ——where a message can be left (on machine or with Nadine) and Sue can return a call at her convenience.

I know that we both appreciate your support in this matter. *The Sun* is trying hard to put the boots to me. Sue meanwhile (according to Svend Robinson) has already moved beyond the matter and regards it as a non-issue—of virtually no importance compared to the real and vital issues and problems we face. She told me tonight she finds the whole business distressful and wants it to end. But *The Sun* will be running another story tomorrow—and the day after that, I've been told.

I was told tonight they intend to investigate my entire past as a journalist and interview editors I have worked with (I was asked to supply names!) and so on, uncovering whatever they can. It seems outrageous…but I learned a long time ago that the media is never more hypocritical than when it rides a vindictively-moral hobbyhorse.

Regards,

John

A phone call clears things up. Sue defends John's intentions but regrets implications...

February 2, 1993

Right to Die Society
Attention: John Hofsess
From: Dennis Kaye

Dear John,

My wife, Ruth, called and spoke with Sue today and I took part in the conversation via our speaker phone. I was disappointed to learn that she has actually seen very little of my correspondence. Over the past couple weeks, I was under the mistaken impression that Sue was taking part in the exchange of information between you and I.

To put things back on an even keel, tomorrow, I'd like you to present all of my past faxes along with your responses so Sue is fully aware of what has transpired thus far. Please forward this letter as well. I trust all the apparent misunderstanding has been in good faith, and hope it doesn't adversely affect the coming appeal.

Sincerely yours,

Dennis Kaye

P.S. I see from your lengthy fax I'll have some good bedtime reading. Glad to hear you're taking everything over to Sue's. Good luck with the media tomorrow.

Tuesday, February 2, 1993

Dear Dennis

I am going out to Sue's in the morning. It's some 17 miles away, far off any bus route, and being a non-driver I am always grateful for a lift. A team of documentary film makers from the CBC will be recording our conversation which I trust will touch upon all the issues we need clarified. I feel the need for an objective record of all that is said. Sue has asked me to bring along our exchanged messages. I had already advised her some days ago of your willingness to make out an affidavit on her behalf and she expressed gratitude for that. I also told her the other day I had sent a cheque to you. But the details of your corre-spondence she has not seen.

I must say that in view of her statement as reported in the press that she has no criticisms to make of any official of the ALS Society of B.C. nor their affidavits that it raises the question as to why she welcomes affidavits from you and Ken Gibbs that do take issue with Rhelda Evans' statements, and quite rightly since they contain inaccu-racies. It is not the only paradox that I must try to resolve tomorrow. My "famous" contract with Sue (Sept. 19) guaranteeing her any help she needs from me unconditionally, makes it clear that she agrees, among other things, that "I hereby authorize Mr. Hofsess to act as my representative and public relations officer in any dealings with the media...I will not grant interviews to any member of the press or electronic media without first consulting with Mr. Hofsess..." and so on. We need to discuss this at length because of late there have been both breaches of the contract and contradictions of it.

I have been working on a draft of a possible Op-Ed article presum-ably for the *Vancouver Sun* dealing expressly with the issues raised. I realize we have never met—and yet I can tell from your writing that you have a commendable strength of mind—and I hope I am not imposing upon you unduly, but I would be interested in your reac-tion, however brief.

Regards,

John

Meeting of the minds…

Attention: Dennis

The conversation with Sue today ran over three hours (and used up 10 videotapes). We talked about everything clear back to the beginning up to where we are now and where we are going and on what terms. Even the crew said they found it emotionally exhausting.

We did not argue, needless to say, and we did not make any major changes in our working relationship. A society member, Helma Libick, has arranged for Sue to have a FAX machine as of Friday and that will greatly facilitate the exchange of information and documents.

There were realizations on both sides that will take some adjusting to. The main one, for me, being that *from this point on* Sue says she will not issue nor authorize any statements criticizing any individual or organization no matter what they do or do not do. She will "turn the other cheek." While this makes her—one might say—more profoundly Christian than her opponents, I cannot help but be disappointed that she will not lend a hand or her name to help correct any social or political problem affecting other terminally ill people. She will concentrate exclusively on her court case and personal life. I accept what she says, of course, but I still wrestle with understanding it. Maybe some forms or phases of illness make a person more self-absorbed than others.

I gave her the file of communiques between us and Allan Graham, etc. I hope that your affidavit will reflect your candid views. The "prolife" forces which dominate the ALS Society of B.C. should not be allowed to prevail—even if Sue now says it is not a matter of concern to her one way or the other. I am arranging for Ken Gibbs to prepare his affidavit shortly.

I am deeply fond of Sue, love her in fact; nothing can change my commitment to her no matter what the legal consequences. But in my heart of hearts—and I hope I can say this in confidence—something died today. I don't know whether it was a part of her or a part of me. For all the immense publicity the case has received there is no sign of political change or organizational growth as a result. Too often the media coverage is confined to the bathos [sic] of Sue's predicament and, without any statements from her encouraging public involvement and political action, she is likely to remain a public figure with no resonance beyond the confines of herself. I realize now that there will be no such public statements from her. I must now learn to forget my disappointment. And until I forget it—to hide it.

Regards,
John

Thursday, February 4, 1993

Dennis Kaye
FAX transmission
From: John Hofsess

Just a quick word.
I heard from Sue a few minutes ago and she said that she will try out her new FAX machine tomorrow morning as soon as it is set up by sending you her first facsimile communication.

She said she has been reviewing our many FAXes this afternoon and has a better appreciation as a result of all the work and ideas involved in seeking a withdrawal of the affidavits.

I will be receiving a *rough draft* of Ken Gibbs' affidavit tomorrow, in anticipation of it being completed next week, and will share it with you if you like.

Hope the trip to Campbell River was not too rough on you.

John

My contribution…

BETWEEN:

SUE RODRIQUEZ [*sic*]

PETITIONER

AND:

ATTORNEY GENERAL OF BRITISH COLUMBIA
ATTORNEY GENERAL OF CANADA

RESPONDENTS

AFFIDAVIT

I, DENNIS KAYE, MAKE OATH AND SAY AS FOLLOWS:

1. I am 37 years of age and am a sufferer of the disease Amyotrophic Lateral Sclerosis commonly referred to as Lou Gehrig's Disease (hereinafter referred to as "ALS").

2. I was diagnosed as having ALS in 1985.

3. Prior to 1985 I was a marine freight operator for about six years and before that worked as a logger in various capacities out of Sayward, British Columbia. I was prior to 1985 approximately 5'10" and weighed about 160 pounds; I now weigh less than 100 pounds.

4. I am now married to Ruth who has been my companion since 1978 and we have two children, Rebecca and Michalla, ages 12 and 8 respectively.

5. My primary reason for swearing this Affidavit is to make known my support for and agreement with the Petitioner in her effort to gain the legal right to an assisted suicide.

6. I also believe that previous statements made to the court by Rhelda Evans are either false or misleading and I refer particularly to her Affidavit which I believe to have been sworn at Vancouver on or about the 17th day of December, 1992 (hereinafter referred to as the "Evans Affidavit").

7. I do not believe that Rhelda Evans suffers from ALS. The Evans Affidavit attempts to leave the impression that people with ALS

are uniformly opposed to the petition of Sue Rodriquez [*sic*].
Since I was diagnosed, I have encountered a number of people
who suffer from ALS. I do not believe that ALS victims share a single view with respect to the relief sought by the Petitioner herein.
ALS does not afflict people of one moral or political persuasion or
belief. I believe that many ALS victims support Sue Rodriquez
[*sic*] in the within matter.

8. ALS affects its victims in a wide variety of ways and as such its victims face and exercise a wide variety of choices particularly with
respect to treatment and living conditions.

9. Some persons with ALS are unable to breathe or eat without
mechanical aid but are able to speak and walk. Others, like
myself, are able, with increasing difficulty, to breathe and swallow
but in my case my speech is unintelligible to most and I am
unable to move anything but my head in anyway approaching a
normal or useful fashion.

10. The Evans Affidavit suggests that a sense of dignity can be
achieved and maintained through psychological counselling. In
my experience there can never be any dignity in having my penis
placed in a bottle day after day, month after month, year after
year so that I can urinate, or in being placed physically onto a toilet from my wheelchair and having myself cleaned by another
person after each bowel movement.

11. The Evans Affidavit suggests that people who have ALS endure
little or no pain. While that statement may be fairly accurate
insofar as physical pain is concerned, it does not recognize the
serious and continuing emotional pain that sufferers of ALS must
endure. It is hard to convey the amount of emotional pain that
one suffers through the indignities hereinbefore referred to, or
in the simple pleasures of life in which one cannot participate, in
such as playing with one's children or even being in a position to
assist one's children should they have an immediate need. One
example of this kind of emotional pain and difficulty was when
I watched one of my children being playfully thrown into the air

by another father and my realization that I could never participate with either of my children in that manner again.

12. In my experience caregivers are often excluded from what we refer to as "life support." When considering life support, tubes, wires and high technology are readily acknowledged as falling within the definition, but each time my wife spoon-feeds me I am reminded that in the true sense of the words I too am on "life support." It is imperative, in my view, that we recognize that discontinuing life support often means much more than pulling a plug or flipping a switch. For some, such as people in my position, the only legal alternative to life support is starvation.

13. I believe it to be a discrimination against physically disabled persons to prevent them from obtaining assistance to do something which is legal for able-bodied persons.

14. In many respects I consider myself to be living the life that the Petitioner wishes to avoid and I have done so for an extended period of time. However, I would not and could not in all good conscience deny the rights which she seeks. I may draw my line in a different place than the Petitioner but what really concerns me and causes me fright is those able-bodied persons who would draw that line for me and for persons in my position and the position of the Petitioner.

15. I have been told by my physician that there has been research conducted with respect to ALS for over 120 years and that to date no cause, cure or treatment to retard its progress has been found. ALS is presently a terminal disease. I believe that people with ALS deserve the legal right to control their own destiny and to have others assist them if that be their desire.

Dennis Kaye

Another rebuttal goes unpublished...

The Editor
FAX transmission
Vancouver Sun

By what right has the *Sun* declared itself judge, jury and executioner of John Hofsess? His crime? He penned Sue Rodriguez's initials at the bottom of an article submitted to Voices (not her signature in a letter, as claimed by the *Sun*) for the sole purpose of protesting against what he regarded as unfair treatment of Ms. Rodriguez.

In representing the article as authored by Ms. Rodriguez, Mr. Hofsess committed an ethical blunder and an error in judgment. But, having admitted he was wrong—in formal apologies to both the reporter concerned and to Ms. Rodriguez—Mr. Hofsess deserves far better than the pernicious character assassination being administered by the *Sun*.

John Hofsess has, almost single-handedly, brought the issue of physician-assisted suicide out of the closet and into the public forum. For that, I think he deserves a lot of credit. He has also been, and continues to be, Ms. Rodriguez's most devoted champion. And for that, he deserves our admiration and our gratitude.

Profile groups have been quick to claim that Mr. Hofsess's action constitutes manipulation of Ms. Rodriguez (Feb. 2 article) but they've been singing that song for months, long before his faux-pas. I'd like to remind these people of a couple of well-known facts: Sue Rodriguez approached The Right to Die Society on her *own* initiative, and she has publicly expressed her desire for a physician-assisted death on many occasions, over several months—and in her own words—most recently in the *Sun*'s January 30 article. In view of these facts, to insist she's being manipulated by anyone is both patronizing and profoundly disrespectful of her. It is also grossly unfair to Mr. Hofsess.

Sue Rodriguez has graciously accepted Mr. Hofsess's apology, with no reservations about his commitment to her. If she can forgive so readily, it would be uncharitable of us to do otherwise. The *Sun* has no right to question her judgment by continuing its public flogging of Mr. Hofsess.

Helma Libick
Member, Right to Die Society of Canada and
Administrative Assistant to Sue Rodriguez

February 11, 1993

FAX Transmission

Dear Dennis

I apologize for not faxing you sooner. I did receive all of the correspondence between you and John. I had no idea you two were so busy with this affidavit stuff.

I have read your affidavit and wish to thank you for your effort in providing the court with this. You definitely will have all ears tuned in. Below is my Fax number.

I hope to keep in touch with you more after this upcoming week. Again, thank you for your support.

Sincerely,
Sue

A ruling comes down from on high…

In court, Sue's lawyer, Chris Considine of Victoria, argued that Section 241(b) violated Sue's right as guaranteed under the Charter of Rights and Freedoms. His argument followed four steps. First, since 1972, suicide has been legal in Canada. But by the time Sue's health deteriorates to a point where she'll want to kill herself, she won't be able to without a doctor's aid. This means the law discriminates against Rodriguez by forcing her—because of her disability—to participate in an illegal act. Considine lost. All three Appeal judges, however, recommended Parliament consider decriminalizing the assisted suicide of terminally ill people.

March 8, 1993

Dear Sue,

I'm sorry things went as they did, and hope that once you've had time to distance yourself from the fray, you'll see that no matter what happens from here on in, by turning one judge, you've already made history.

Your spirit continues to inspire me.

A like-minded friend,

Dennis Kaye

P.S. For what it's worth, I hope my affidavit served some purpose.

Mr. Dennis Kaye

Dear Dennis,

Thank you for your kind note of March 8. You said you hoped I had managed to "distance myself from the fray." Obviously not—as you may have gathered from the latest publicity. But I'm still hanging in there and continue to draw strength from people like you who remind me that I'm not alone in this.

I want to again thank you for your efforts in producing the affidavit. I *know* it wasn't an easy task for you physically (or emotionally?). But you can rest assured that it did indeed serve its purpose since it was submitted as evidence to the B.C. Court of Appeal and the judges would have read it as part of the materials submitted for the hearing.

You probably won't have any use for it (since faxing is so much easier) but I just want to draw your attention to my new mailing address (above).

Warm regards,

Sue Rodriguez

The last word goes to Sue...

Dear Dennis,

I appreciate your inviting me to provide closing comments to your chapter.

The affidavit controversy now seems very distant to me; so much has happened since then. I do clearly remember how shocked I was that day in court, when it first appeared that a representative of the ALS Society had filed an affidavit opposing my petition. While I hadn't expected the Society to support me, neither did I anticipate its opposition. But when I learned who had submitted the affidavit, I realized that this person didn't represent the Society's position; conversations with other ALS Society members make it obvious that there was a spectrum of opinions on this issue.

The matter was being addressed by my lawyer, and steps were being taken to make it clear to the court that her affidavit did not represent the position of the ALS Society—when the matter suddenly became a media event. No, I was not happy about Rhelda Evans's actions, but I made no public statement about them, nor was I responsible for the various inflammatory statements made in various newspaper articles. That simply is not my style.

And it was fundamental differences in personal style that were the reason for my subsequent dissociation from The Right to Die Society of Canada, not philosophical differences. Then as now, I firmly believe in the Society's objectives; I admire John Hofsess's devotion to the right-to-die issue, and I deeply appreciate the commitment he made to me. However, over time, it became obvious that his approach and mine were incompatible on too many issues for him to continue to act as my representative. It was a very painful decision to make but, on this sensitive issue, I had to be able to speak for myself, in my own way.

Sue Rodriguez

238   **Laugh, I Thought I'd Die**

In May, 1993, the case was brought before the Supreme Court of Canada. After four months a panel of nine judges deliberated and on September 30 a verdict was handed down. By a margin of one vote, Sue's request was denied.

If there were an eleventh
commandment, it would probably be
"thou shalt not attempt
philosophy in thy first book."
But in all likelihood, this will be
my first and last literary effort,
so I've decided to go for it anyway.

20

Will the Real God Please Stand Up

I was baptized as an infant. A man in a dress, who I didn't know from Adam, dumped some water on my head, said some stuff and declared me whatever it is they declare. Aside from these blessed beginnings my upbringing was non-religious, so the next few pages are born out of a theological naivety which I freely admit. This chapter is neither an attempt to proselytize for nor to chastise any faith in particular. Nor is it my intention to incite rebuttal. I simply wish to shed some light on the behaviour of "the religious zealot" as it relates to one terminally ill person...namely me. Just think of it as one happy heathen's way of getting a word in edgewise.

Let me take you on a brief imaginary journey now...a journey from no particular starting point. I have been walking for what seems like years: up back streets, down side roads, under bridges, over bridges. I'm searching for something very small and very important. Even though I'm not exactly sure what "it" is, I am confident that I'll know "it" when I see it.

I have no clear memory of when this journey began, only that it was a long—no, make that a very long time ago. Most recently I've been walking along a winding seaside road. Ahead, as far as the eye can see, it traces an irregular coastline into the distance. Behind me, it does the same. Below and to my right, giant waves pound a long and windswept sandy shore. Mile after mile they pound. Countless waves. How many? As days go by…thousands.

To my left, ancient weather-beaten trees twist and turn against the elements. Mile after mile they grow. Countless trees. How many? As days go by…millions.

On every tree, colourful leaves shimmer in the wind. Mile after mile they shimmer. Countless leaves. How many? As days go by…billions.

Tiring of the road, I take a meandering path down to the water's edge and continue walking by the sea. Glittering brilliantly beneath my feet are countless grains of sand. How many? As days go by…trillions.

I keep on walking. One more day. One more night. One more morning. Finally, on this particular morning, a weary sun creeps into a cloudless sky and I feel so far from home. But wait! Up ahead and directly in my path, something is sticking straight up in the sand, and I sense my journey nearing an end. Each step brings me closer to my objective. As I draw near, the thing in the sand turns out to be a shovel, but not just any shovel. Engraved on its handle, in an ancient dialect, are the words, "Sacred Shovel." (In my imaginary journeys I can decipher ancient dialects.)

Naturally, I do what comes naturally. I dig. Down a few million grains worth (about a foot), I uncover a sight to behold! There before me, gleaming like a precious jewel, is a singularly special grain of sand. Surely this is not just any grain of sand. As I gaze down on its granular grandeur, it all starts to come clear. During my years of walking, I'd often wondered why all I had in my pockets was a magnifying glass and a pair of tweezers. What could be more obvious? With tweezers in hand, I bend down and gently pluck the tiny gem. Brimming with anticipation, I raise it up and fix my glass on it. Instantly I realize I am holding something truly holy. It's the strongest grain of sand on earth, impervious to a thousand powerful waves. It's the oldest grain of sand on earth, older than a million ancient trees. It's the most colourful grain of sand on earth, more beautiful than a billion colourful leaves. And as you might expect, it turns out to be the most brilliant grain of sand on earth, its heavenly hue more brilliant by far than any of the other trillions. I see the light!

The longer I look, the more it reveals. As I peer into its deceivingly fragile loveliness, I'm amazed to see how perfectly round it is. When I look closer, I'm even more amazed to see that parts of it are covered with crystalline blue water. Other parts are textured in earth tones, like tiny continents. To my utter disbelief, I appear to be holding a miniature Earth! Can you imagine? Sure enough, as I look still closer, there are eensy-weensy waves pounding an itty-bitty beach, bordered all along with teeny-tiny trees. And as you may have guessed...standing by an infinitesimal shovel, on the itty-bitty beach, is a minuscule man holding a microscopic magnifying glass and, yes, the teensiest weensiest tweezers you ever saw.

It's unfortunate, but even imaginary magnifying glasses have their limits. If mine had been just a bit more powerful, you might guess that I would have seen the minuscule man holding an Earth-shaped grain of subatomic sand. But try as I might, I couldn't quite make out what my pint-size counterpart had in his tweezers. It doesn't really matter, though. I'm convinced there was absolutely nothing there. How could there be? How could he possibly be holding a miniature Earth, when my miniature Earth was the only miniature Earth on Earth? I had seen the light. So what if I'd only seen a trillionth of the Earth? So what if the trillions of grains I'd seen were only a trillionth of what there was to see? I didn't have to see any more. I had seen the light. I had reached my journey's end.

Admittedly, the notion of a journey like this being true may be absurd, but what strikes me as more absurd is that bright, educated adults openly embrace proportionately similar ideas, and often look on those who don't as poor misguided souls. In the grand scheme of things, a worm has intelligence, but a chicken has more. The same thing goes for dogs who are less intelligent than apes. And even though dolphins are pretty darn smart, on good days we're smarter. Somebody has to be at the top of the intellectual heap. But we seem to be the only species arrogant enough to claim God-given dominion over what amounts to little more than a galactic grain of sand.

I had no way of knowing that following my diagnosis a barrage of unsolicited religious pitches from zealots of every description would come to colour my thoughts. Regardless of where on the religious rainbow my sentiments may have lain, once word of my illness got around, members of every shade seemed to converge on me. It may go without saying, but hearing I had a killer disease forced me to confront personal frailties I never knew existed. My mind quickly became cluttered with a myriad of things: funeral expenses, loss of income, which goals to meet and which to let slide. Was it worth setting goals at all? Why did they wait till after I got sick to invent bungee jumping? It was a very confusing time. Unfortunately, in the midst of all this confusion, I was seen as fair game by every religion under the sun.

Believe in my God!
No, believe in my God!
No, over here, my God is best!
You're forgiven!
Have faith!
You're a sinner!
Repent!
Convert!
Be healed!
Hallafrigginluia already!!!

What exactly draws the zealot? I'm still not sure. It's as if once you receive a terminal diagnosis you start emitting some sort of homing frequency only they can hear...a kind of religious dog whistle. Some would hover like bees over honey; others seemed to circle like birds over carrion. But no matter the angle of approach, once these vendors of truth came in for a landing, most of them were incapable of presenting themselves honestly. Their initial pretense in almost every case was that they had something they wanted to share with me, but the more they talked, the more I realized the "sharing" they had in mind was in fact an obligation—they had no choice in the matter. Coming to my emotional rescue was perceived to be a prerequisite to their own salvation.

I think most of us find it hard to think of our mortality without at least pondering the question of spirituality. For the atheist, there may be no questions worth answering. For the spiritually self-secure there may be no answers worth questioning. But for many, myself included, spirituality is best left undefined. In a world of quick fixes and pat answers, it's the things that defy definition that keep life interesting.

Don't mistake my lack of reverence for disrespect. It's just that religion, like most things, has different effects on different people. For some it seems to have a calming effect. For others it appears to produce an adrenaline-like rush. I've seen it swing people in both directions so I'm reluctant to generalize. But no matter what form the euphoria takes, nothing I said or did seemed to alter the allegiance any zealot held for his or her particular train of thought. It was as if, by accepting one idea, they had somehow lost the ability to consider others. Regardless of which doctrine was being conveyed, I noticed these zealots seemed to have a few things in common.

Common Zealot Traits:
- they take for granted that because you're dying, you must be in need of spiritual guidance
- they invariably believe their God to be the only true God, their truth to be the only truth and their interpretation of both to be the only valid interpretation
- they believe that without the acceptance of their faith and their faith alone, your death will be, at best, meaningless, or at worst, eternally painful
- their belief in the first three traits is so firm that they adamantly deny any negative effects their preaching may have
- they regularly belittle the beliefs of other zealots

When I first started this chapter I had a pompous notion that, with a little bit of research, I might find a rational explanation for why zealots act so weird, thereby justifying my disdain for same. I thought there might be some less obvious commonality, like a hormonal imbalance or too much oat bran or something. But my trip to the library made for a rude awakening. At first glance the theology section was an ideal world where mythical kings and modern-day messiahs stood shoulder to shoulder on the same shelf. Tribal lords and animal spirits danced together without incident, and there were more "one true Gods" than you could shake a stick at.

Unfortunately, it was also a nebulous world where symbolism and realism overlapped far too often to offer a poor dying guy like me any real peace of mind. I obviously wasn't the only one who was confused, and after about sixty seconds in the presence of all those fat musty books I started to feel intimidated. I got an eerie feeling that if I stayed there too long I might get an irresistible urge to shave my head or hand out leaflets on the street corner.

By the time all the smoke and incense cleared I had abandoned the idea of psychoanalysing the zealot and chose instead to take a closer look at myself. Why did I feel so threatened in the first place? Over and over I found myself drawing parallels between my own peace of mind and that of my children. It may sound selfish, but the closer death gets, the more I'm coming to see my daughters as extensions of myself. ALS renders me incapable of protecting their physical future, so it's entirely possible I've become oversensitive about protecting their spiritual sovereignty.

If only the world were as quiet and orderly as the library first appeared, but that's hardly the case. From the subtle sound of snide remarks to the unholy thunder of so-called holy wars, inter-religious disharmony is alive and well. Globally, from the ever-shifting sands of the Middle East to the blood-stained borders of Europe, Moslems, Christians, Jews and Gentiles continue to hammer away at one another ad nauseam. Locally, I hear the under-the-breath mutterings of Catholics dumping on Protestants, Jehovah's Witnesses dumping on Catholics, Baptists dumping on Jehovah's Witnesses, and so on, and so on, and so on. How then, in all good conscience, can I walk a young, impressionable child into this kind of ideological lions' den?

There's an especially interesting concept of creation held by some Ethiopians, who also believe themselves to be God's chosen people. According to them, God moulded the first men from clay. He put the first batch in the oven to bake but left them too long. They came out burnt and black, so he threw them away to the south of Africa. He took the second batch out too soon and they were pasty white, so he threw them away to the north where they became Arabs and Europeans. The third batch came out just right and he put them in Ethiopia.

I take it from my limited biblical knowledge that western religions see things very differently. According to them, it all started with two people…not Hop Sing and Kim Soo, not Fritz and Olga, but Adam and Eve. Neither one is said to have had proper birth-parents like you and I. From the moment they were conjured up, they were full grown, properly plumbed and pre-programmed to populate a planet. And whereas aboriginal peoples commonly have us descending from animals, more educated theologians have it that animals walked two by two into a really, really, really big boat and in fact owe their survival to a family man from somewhere around the Mediterranean. If I have the rest of the story right, after every species known to man was present and accounted for, it started to rain and forty days later the earth was underwater. Normally I'm not one to split hairs, but I did a little calculating and covering the earth in forty days means it rained over five hundred feet every day, everywhere, simultaneously. Considering the historical record for one day's rainfall is less than twenty-four inches, either somebody made an editorial booboo of biblical proportion, or God has a more twisted sense of humour than he gets credit for.

Perhaps if I'd taken up a religious interest in my youth, or had had one imposed on me by my parents…maybe then I'd find it easier to pass on concepts like these to my girls. It would be so much easier if the concepts were all as innocent as Ethiopian people-cookies and floating zoos, but I'm afraid it gets worse. Zealot after zealot insisted that if I didn't adopt this religion or that religion, I'd be nothing more than dead meat in the eyes of God. Some said I was destined to roast in hell. Others insisted there was no hell, but I'd miss out on an everlasting utopia reserved especially for them. These dooms-day zealots universally maintain that fire and brimstone are God's pre-planned answers to our social and spiritual deterio-ration...the ultimate ethnic cleansing. Holocaust, Doomsday, Armageddon, Judgment Day, hell or no hell, this is where I have to draw the line.

Since getting ALS I find myself searching more and more for good news. I may be terminally ill, but I'm also terminally optimistic, and in the face of scorched-earth prophecies like these, it's simply impossible to acknowledge social, let alone spiritual advancements as anything but meaningless skid marks on an otherwise unstoppable careen into eternal damnation. If I am to believe with all my heart that things are predestined to get worse before they can get better, no amount of earthly improvement will ever satisfy me in the here and now. In my here and now (today in fact) I hear the anguished pleas of another parent whose child has fallen prey to yet another sexual ghoul...another day...another broad-cast...another deviant slithers into court wearing a coat for a hat. The optimist in me sees images like these as irrefutably positive; a mere decade ago, child-molesters could rely on society's silence. But somehow the doomsday zealot interprets even exposures like these as further evidence of impending retribution.

To justify my optimism, once again I found myself draw-ing parallels that included my children. Aided by an abstract series of historic photographs, I compared the lives of my girls to those of children in days gone by, and without excep-tion, each comparison served to reinforce my assertion that they will indeed see better days than I. In the first image I saw a nine-year-old boy in a soiled blue military uniform. His parade drum hangs low. Before him, what's left of a Confederate soldier lies face down in a sickening mixture of earth and blood. It's 1863. If that boy could see his twentieth-century counterpart waging mock war on the liquid-crystal battlefield of a plastic video toy, would he long for his past or for our future?

Next I stepped forward to the turn of the century. The image: a one-room, dirt-floor shack in southern Georgia. A weary black man and his weary black wife are praying for all they're worth. The dark, vacant eyes of their thirteen children betray the typhoid that will eventually take them all. If they could see their twentieth-century counterparts, would they long for their time or ours?

Another image took me back eighty years and a half mile straight down. A young boy with an old man's cough chips away at life in the dusty bowels of a Welsh coal mine. He is not alone. Even with today's shortage of day-care, given the choice, would that boy be willing to tough it out in the nineties?

In a final image, the grime of black coal is contrasted by the stark, white monotony of an overcrowded asylum. It's 1939. Around a large, dimly lit ward are dozens of forgotten souls in various states of mental disarray. On a dank, urine-soaked mattress, an emotionally scattered girl seems to be contemplating her relativity as best she can. If she could see just one generation into her future, what would cross her untapped mind? If she were capable of rational thought, would she see today's Special Olympians as further evidence of our sacrilegious spiral toward Armageddon?

It would be asinine to present imagery like this strictly in its past tense. Children still fall victim to war, disease, forced labour and institutional abuse, but in each case, the rules of the past are gradually becoming the exceptions of the present.

There must be some lofty Freudian principle to explain

why I keep reaching these rose-coloured conclusions. Cliché as it may sound, I think my aversion to organized pessimism may stem, at least in part, from a childhood experience of my own. When I was a kid in Victoria, I remember riding my bicycle past a tall wooden fence on Cook Street. Its vertical boards (about ten feet high) ran for an entire city block. Between each board was a long, narrow crack, and no normal boy could ride the length of that fence without stopping at least once to peer through. The view between any two boards was restricted, but if you stopped enough times you could piece together a composite image of a well-groomed athletic park on the other side. By today's multi-million-dollar sports standards it wasn't much—just your basic soccer field, a matching set of goal posts and some wooden bleachers—but to a scuff-toed kid in the early sixties it was as big as all Saskatchewan.

To put my hickish sense of wonder in context, it would probably help to know I was born on Saltspring Island. Before Saltspring was taken over by the rurally-minded masses, it was a gentle and genuine world apart. Local milk from local cows was still delivered by local farmers, all twelve school grades fit under one roof, and a free flow of gossip was still maintained by means of an outdated hand-crank phone system.

It was a great place to be growing up, but when I was nine my mother unexpectedly packed up my sister and I and the three of us moved to "the big city." She and my father had just split up, and the sudden change didn't come without a certain amount of culture shock. Dial telephones were a brief novelty, and the change in schools went okay. I even learned to like the wimpy creamless milk that came in cardboard boxes. But I was ill-prepared for the city's relentless onslaught of traffic. On Saltspring, passing cars had never been more than periodic intrusions into an otherwise quiet country boyhood. But in direct contrast, Victoria's non-stop stream of humanity produced an incessant and unnerving hum that took some getting used to. Silence had become a memory overnight, but with a little imagination, when I stood at that fence and looked down the length of that field, I found I could tune out the hum. Some days it would vaporize in the heat of an open prairie. Other days it would crystallize in the frigid stillness of an endless arctic tundra. Still other days, when my juvenile juices were really flowing, the traffic would simply de-materialize and settle like dust over some distant lunar seabed.

One afternoon, while riding across town in my uncle's pick-up, I learned there was another way of looking at things. I vaguely recall my face pressed up against the passenger window as we sped along Cook Street, but if the day's details are sketchy, my memory of what happened next is not. As the world flew by my nose, I quite literally snapped to attention. When we passed my field of dreams, the sudden and unexpected optical effect of all those cracks flashing by combined to form a fleeting, albeit blurry image of the entire field. For a few brief seconds the fence seemed to vanish. For a few brief seconds I could see it all!

Even on days when games had been in progress, players had always slipped in and out of view too quickly for me to follow what was going on…but not that day. Everything was there: goal posts, bleachers, players running, even a black-and-white soccer ball flying though the air. There's a technical term for what I saw, and I know everybody's seen something similar at some point, but in the excitement of the moment I mistakenly thought of the experience as my own personal revelation…which unfortunately lands me right back in the realm of the religious zealot.

Thirty years later, that fence has become a metaphor for the barriers that prevent us all from seeing the big picture. Some of us dwell on a single crack or viewpoint to the exclusion of all else. Others prefer to glimpse life from as many viewpoints as time allows. To surrender one's entire thought process to a single doctrine or ideology, however tempting, is to squander the miracle right under our noses. If reality isn't miraculous enough for you, you probably aren't looking hard enough. It all puts me in mind of the dyslexic, agnostic insomniac who lay awake nights wondering if there really was a Dog. What each of us see, believe we see, or refuse to see does not and will not alter what is. And as for our children, regardless of faith, if we confine them to blinkered or exclusionary viewpoints from birth, it only stands to reason they will come to accept intolerance toward others as perfectly normal. As they grow, the success of everything, from the friendships they form to the mates they choose, will ultimately depend on the ability of others to measure up. They need not think the way we think. Rather, they need only understand why we think as we do, judge if they must, then use that understanding to develop ways of thinking for themselves.

Since getting ALS I've connected with many warm and kind-hearted people (religious and otherwise), but only when they gave of "their" spirit could I call it genuine kindness, unqualified kindness…love. I've yet to get that warm feeling from a zealot. If it turns out there's no afterlife I'll be as pissed off as the next guy. I just hope they don't get too upset if they get to wherever they're going and find out I'm already there. In the meantime, no one else can live my life and no one else can die my death.

It's hard to see the truth with a lot of people blocking your view, and it's hard to hear the truth with a lot of voices ringing in your ears. Sometimes I think I'm still just a child at a crack in the fence trying to block out the hum. Who knows? Maybe we all are.

A lot has changed since D-Day.
I have lived to see one Canadian woman
orbit the Earth, another chair
the House of Commons and yet another
claim the keys to 24 Sussex Drive.
I've seen old walls fall, new nations rise,
Big Macs in Moscow, and, hey,
how 'bout those Jays?
Mick Jagger is a grandfather for crying
out loud——I may be dying young,
but there comes a point when
you have to admit you're getting old.

21

I'm Pecking As Fast As I Can

I had one major problem writing this book. It was my inability to master that precious period between the time I would get an idea and the time I'd finally get it on paper. When the average writer (if there is such a thing) feels the inspirational floodgates opening, they can hop on their keyboard and ride the wave until its momentum evaporates. But when I get inspired the wave just rolls right over me, and until someone props me up in front of my laptop I can only hope I've absorbed enough water to whet the reader's appetite.

It wouldn't be so bad if my best ideas didn't invariably materialize when I'm trapped in bed. There seems to be a predictable, almost uncanny relationship between the poignancy of my thoughts and the distance to my computer. If I didn't know better, I'd swear my mind had a mind of its own. Often I struggle for hours, even days, trying to figure out the best way to make a particular point or get some critical message across. Then the second my head hits the pillow—eureka! But until I'm within pecking distance, all I can do is file the idea away with all the other eurekas and hope it's still there when I need it. As time has gone by, my idea inventory has built to a point where the only way I can remember something new is to forget something old. If I had a mind like Stephen Hawking's I'm sure I'd have a big, fat impressive-looking volume by now, but with my limited capacity, I'm afraid I've forgotten almost as much as I've written.

To make matters worse, as time goes by, the more I type, the slower and less accurate I become. You have to remember that in my case, typing means wearing a stupid-looking contraption on my head. Every last letter, space, shift and return means bobbing my head up and down, or more accurately, down and up. Not surprisingly, all this bobbing brings on neck spasms which repeatedly cause me to miss the keys I'm aiming for. As the spasms get more and more frequent, my mistakes get more and more frequent. Between hitting the wrong keys, backspacing, deleting and correcting, I often have to bob eight or nine times for a three-letter word. Conservatively, not counting rewrites and editing, I figure I've got at least half a million bobs invested so far, and the closer I get to the end of the book, the more weak my neck becomes. Through it all, I've been haunted by the thought that I might get to the last word, of the last sentence, on the very last page, and   not   have   q uite   enough

Just kidding! I do worry though...not so much about whether or not I'll finish my book, but about how my body may react when I finally do. What if I can't stop bobbing? What if I strike the final key, and my head just keeps jerking up and down like one of those over-heated terriers that can't stop humping? When the guys in the fancy station wagon come to cart me off, maybe they'll have to strap my head to the gurney just to be on the safe side. I hope I don't unnerve anyone at the funeral parlour. With a little luck they'll just think it's somebody knocking at the door! But hey, first things first.

As time ticks on, I find I'm thinking a lot more about the past than about the future. I look back with some embarrassment at the early days, my frantic search for answers, and how quick I was to accept the advice of others. "You ought to give this a try, Dennis." "You've got to try that, Dennis." Acupuncture, acupressure, tissue salts, urine therapy, creative visualization, specific adjustment, prayer, radical fasting, positive thinking, telepathic gem therapy, not to mention a variety of wonder teas, muscle-building powders and stinky protein concoctions. Come to think of it, there was even one of those new-age seminar types convinced she need only lay her hands on me and all my problems would be over. But when she looked me straight in the eye and said it would cost fifty dollars, I said, "Thanks, but no thanks."

Early in the search I even let a chiropractor have a go at me, but he was convinced that all I had was tennis elbow. I've often thought it would be a hoot to go back and pay that guy a visit sometime, preferably when his waiting room is really crowded. Wearing nothing but hospital pyjamas and my bionic-looking headset, I'd carefully manoeuvre my cumbersome, voice-equipped powerchair up to the reception desk. Then, with just enough drool for effect, I'd peer accusingly over my chest-level communicator and with volume on high

I'd peck out, "The tennis elbow's gone, but you've definitely got some explaining to do."

Not everything has been futile. In my more recent past something far more positive happened. Our house is on the edge of a steep cliff that's on the edge of a secluded cove that's on the edge of a semi-sheltered bay. When I'm at the edge of our sundeck I can look right down into the water, and early this spring, I received what can only be described as a natural gift. I was just biding my time between ideas, and, as is my habit, I was trying to sort out some of the more perplexing secrets of the universe: Is "nothing" a noun? Are pigeons really polar-bear toed? You know. Ironically, I had just started to calculate (in my head) how much raw sewage fish are responsible for when something truly special broke my concentration.

Out in the bay, herring had begun to school—great swirling balls of life that marked the passing of one more season, but more than that, seemed to confirm my own tenuous place in yet another earthbound cycle. Those boiling masses of fish turned out to be a living precursor to a wondrous marine display that lasted almost three days.

Seagulls and arctic terns came first. Their aerial jousting and incessant peels heralded the coming advance. Then came the eagles—more and more of them, until they easily numbered over a hundred. No sooner would these bald-headed beauties arrive than they'd launch an assault, scattering the smaller birds with all the bluff and bravado of schoolyard bullies. A handful of great blue herons came next and took their places on the tide flats below...followed by an Orca cow with two young calves! Compared to the gulls, the whales' approach was downright lazy, and for a couple hours each afternoon, our bay became their private trough. After that, everything seemed to come in twos: sea lions, seals, cormorants, as well as a variety of ducks and other seabirds that I don't know the names of. Even a pair of Canada geese dropped in to see what all the fuss was about. And like our resident sea loons, the geese chose to keep their distance, content to squawk and coo encouragement from the sidelines.

Even for someone who has spent most of his life around the water, it was an inspiration. At its peak, the whole scene changed from one of frenzy, greed and pandemonium to one of harmony and balance. It was spring itself—everything in its place—each creature keeping time to a universal pulse. Even the unseen carnage below the surface seemed to be part of something perfect, and I felt a part of that perfection. The sea was alive. The air was alive. And as sappy as it sounds, I felt more alive than I had in years.

As for my future, I've never been one to put much stock in predictions, but of course that's never stopped me from making them either. Since starting this book I've had to put some really promising projects on the back-burner. Maybe now I'll find the time, and a like-minded sugar daddy, so I can get something exciting happening. On the other hand, even though my neck doesn't have another book in it, you never know what the technology wunderkinds will come up with next. I might just luck into one of those fancy new sight-sensitive communication systems and blink out a sequel. Then again, maybe I'll just bow to temptation and start sleeping in until bedtime...NOT! I've finally reached the irreversible conclusion that no matter what accomplishments or failures the future may bring, it's better to be a sick has-been than a healthy wannabe.

I suppose all that leaves is the present. I think I must have subconsciously saved it for last so I'd have an easy way of comparing the way I feel now to the way I felt when I pecked out my first paragraph. To look at me, you'd probably say that there is no comparison. Every day is a bad hair day. My body, or what's left of it, is literally starting to fall apart. This morning I sneezed and all hell broke loose. My pecker flew off (the one on my head), somewhere behind the bridge of my nose I felt my pupils cross paths, and just before my ears popped I swear I heard the sickening thud of my colon bouncing off the back of my dentures. Surprisingly though, aside from the obvious physical stuff and a few personal priorities, not that much has really changed.

I still have my dog. Remember my dog? I said in my first "Morningside" letter that I probably wouldn't outlive him. Well, in human years, Shad's pushing a hundred now. His whiskers have all turned grey, he's gone as deaf as a post, and the way he struggles to his feet after a nap makes me think I might have spoken too soon. Just the other day I was parked out on the sundeck. A few feet away, Shad's big, black, Newfie carcass was sprawled out like someone told him it was a dog's life and he'd taken them seriously. He's always been a couple kibbles short of a bag, but on this particular day, he was right out to lunch. Anyway, midway between the blue of my eye and the blue of the sky, I noticed a big turkey-vulture had started to carve slow, ominous circles overhead, and I couldn't help but wonder which one of us it had its eye on. As it circled it occurred to me that, at least in my case, ALS is a lot like that bird—ready to capitalize on my every weakness, but patient enough to leave me with the illusion of control.

Immanuel Kant, an eighteenth-century philosopher, once said, "Happiness is not an ideal of reason but of imagination." Well I am here to say that Immanuel Kant didn't know his wing-nut from a hole in the ground. My happiness is not imaginary. The economic analysts can put me below whatever poverty line they choose. The nuclear fatalists can block out my sun with mushroom clouds. The ecologists can shoot my sky full of holes. And the environmentalists can acid rain all over my parade. When all the number-crunching, sign-waving, book-thumping congregations have gotten their licks in, I will still be smiling.

Am I getting out just in time? I think not. Should I feel grateful for having been blessed with a fatal disease? I think not. Must I apologize for being happy? I think not. Sometimes I wish I could just jump up out of my chair, wipe the spit from my chin and yell at the top of my under-inflated lungs, "I'm happy as hell and I'm not going to take it any more! I am invalid, hear me roar. I twitch, therefore I am."

I may find it hard to swallow and think at the same time, but I can still enjoy the smell of fresh split cedar, the sight of shooting stars and the feel of my daughters' goodnight kisses. I still get that comfortable feeling when I hear the sound of a hard rain on our roof. I still like my coffee strong, my liquor straight, and whenever Ruth is foolish enough to feed me baked beans, I'm still a force to be reckoned with. If you're able to look beyond the superficial things, ALS isn't so tough. Oh sure, it's won almost every battle so far. It's robbed my girls of things they won't fully understand until they have children of their own. It continues to deny Ruth the simple freedom to come and go as she pleases. It's stripped me of my independence. And yes, unless something miraculous happens, it will kill me. But as strange as it may sound, I can honestly say I no longer think of my disease as a worthy opponent.

There's still love in our home, often joy, and rarely a day without laughter. All things considered, when I put ALS up against the things in life that really count, it doesn't stand a chance.

Acknowledgments

Beyond my immediate family, over the years there were many whose kindness and support, in one way or another, inspired me to keep on pecking. The roles of some were fleeting. Others seemed to be there every step of the way. They all deserve more than just my thanks, but until I'm rich and famous, that's all they get.

In no particular order…

David Broadland—for everything, including the advice to write a book.

My Fairy Grandmother—for waving your wand whenever things got rough.

Ray and Virginia Brown—for helping and helping and helping and

helping and…

Peter Gzowski—for putting your microphone where your mouth is.

Pia Persson—for blisters.

David Zamluk—for a kick in the ass when I needed it most.

Eric Mairs—for keeping me in touch and in tunes.

Dennis Berntson—for keeping the sharks away.

Harvey Kane—for inspiration.

Tom Whitfield—for Radar Hill.

George Wiebe—for sharing that special someone.

René and Betty Roh—for a lasting friendship.

Hilary Stewart—for making me feel like a real live writer.

Tassila Brown—for being so patient.

Amyotrophic Lateral Sclerosis Society—for lots and lots of stuff.

Muscular Dystrophy Association—for lots and lots of other stuff.

John Hofsess—for keeping me in interesting reading material.

G.F. Strong ALS Team—for just being there.

Karyn Ruel—for raising the soft-boiled egg to a culinary art form.

Sue Christiaens—for treating me like more than a number.

Neil Beveridge—for putting a friendly face on the system.

Donna Williams—for a lesson in courage.

Art Bobrick—for putting your back into it.

Carl and Sue Fossum—for a laptop in the nick of time.

Jackie Sutcliff—for standing behind me. I love it when you push me around.

Bly Kaye—for pitching in to make something special even more special.

Quadra Islanders—for big hearted small-town spirit.

Garry Grant—for bringing the Triumph back for one last burn.

Mo Davenport—for finally taking a drop in pay.

Dave Rose—for lending a hand in difficult times.

Evy McDonald—for beating the odds.

Dr. Tom Perry—for the vote of confidence.

Roy and Wendy Slater—for volunteer spirit.

Barry Houlihan—for a puck-n-good time.

Marc Crane—for bending the rules.

Mike Richmond—for all the favours.

Phil Hicks—for all the yuks.

Dane Simoes—for all the freebies.

The Kelsey Bay Firewood and BBQ Brigade—for the firewood and the BBQ.

Maarten and Nadine Schaddelee—for coming through when it counted most.

Jane Little—for that summer by the lake (sigh).

Jim MacKenzie—for clearing the air.

Phil Bissel—for doing the right thing.

Sarah Ferguson—for considering what so many others wouldn't.

Rick Hansen—for the nod of encouragement.

Carter Zigmunt—for turning ideas into reality.

BCTV—for breaking with tradition.

Karla Mebbs—for opening doors.

Greg Danbrook—for enough laughs to last a lifetime.